Good Morning Sunshine

A Daily Devotional

By

Dianna Stone

Dedication

Good Morning Sunshine is dedicated to my husband, MTS, and my children and grandchildren, who are my Sunshine. Special thanks to all of those who believed in me and urged me to publish my daily musings! More than anything, I give thanks to God for blessing me more than I could have ever imagined.

About the Author

Life is full of God's goodness and there is always something to be thankful for. When circumstances seem overwhelming and dark, there is a Light that will provide peace, assurance and guidance in the midst of chaos. It is possible to hang onto your peace and let nothing steal your joy. Starting your day off with a word of encouragement and recognizing the presence of God can change your perspective and alter your daily outlook on life.

Dianna Stone is a clergyperson, wife, mother, and grandmother. She is passionate about sharing joy and encouragement and pointing others to find goodness in God, in the world, and within themselves. Good Morning Sunshine is a light that shines and provides direction to hope, grace, and purpose.

Table of Contents

January

January 1

Good Morning Sunshine! Happy New Year! Make it a day of Promise that turns into a year, or a lifetime, of Promise. We make resolutions on New Year's Eve; we tell ourselves we are going to be different; we are going to change who we currently are to become better. We resolve to eat better, act better, think better, be better organized, and we start out with the best of intentions, and soon enough, for most of us, we go back to our old lifestyle. The result, disappointment, guilt, or even apathy; we just stop caring. We move on and basically just decide or choose that the old way of life is acceptable, and if it doesn't go well, next year this time we will resolve to do it differently again. What if we lived with Promise rather than resolutions? Scripture is full of God's promises. Aren't we blessed that our God doesn't make resolutions that are broken but provides us with promises of making all things new, promises of hope for better days, of peace and no fear, promises that we are not alone and that we are loved beyond measure? What if we held onto these promises and asked God to guide us to become better, to become who God has created us to be. Let's live this New Year with God's Promises and with our own promises rather than resolutions and Enjoy!

January 2

Good Morning Sunshine! Make it a Day of Positive Influence. Do you realize the number of people you come into contact with each day? It's more than you realize because we don't necessarily think about or keep a tally of everyone we encounter. There are so many ways we come across others; some by phone, some in person, some via email or internet, and some we pass by on the sidewalk, drive alongside on the highway or shop within the market. With this in mind, you should realize that you have been given a gift, the gift to touch the lives of others. You do it whether you know it or not, but do you know if your influence on them is positive or negative? Your impact on others doesn't mean you'll be spending hours showering wisdom upon someone or investing all of your time into one person. Your influence can be as simple as a kind word, a listening ear, a sympathetic response, a gentle touch, helping someone in need, or even a smile. Your influence is your life; how are you living? What you do and how you live influence others. Make today awesome! Live a positive life and Enjoy!

January 3

Good Morning Sunshine! Make it a Day of Claiming! When a person wins the latest lottery jackpot, they have to come forward to claim their winnings. They had to claim it before they could receive it. Well, my friends, congratulations! You've won the lottery. Wait, what? I know your bank account didn't grow overnight; how did you win the lottery? Glad you asked. You've won because you have received all that money can't buy and more than a bank account can hold. You have been given mercy, grace, forgiveness, compassion, joy, happiness, love, and peace. You can't buy them, but you certainly can claim them. All are available to you, and all you have to do is claim them. Yup, it's that simple. Hanging onto it, well, that's where the hard part comes in, but all of this belongs to you through Jesus Christ. Claim it, hold onto it and Enjoy!

January 4

Good Morning Sunshine! Make it a Day of Losing Control. Oh wait, in order to lose something, it would mean that you had to have it in the first place. Don't you wish there were moments when you could stop time, change your circumstances, and manipulate the outcome of any situation to go in your favor and have control over every aspect of your life? Sure, we all do, but that's not realistic. So many situations and obstacles may present themselves that were completely out of our control. The truth is the only thing we can change, and control is our approach, our response, and our attitude. This is not always that easy when things don't go our way. However, when we relinquish what we believe is our control to God, who is ultimately in control, we very often realize God's plan for us is far better than we could have imagined. Lose control today. Have an open heart, an open mind, and a willing, peaceful spirit, and make it a knowing God is in control kind of day! Enjoy!

January 5

Good Morning Sunshine! Make it a day of Dieting! Seriously, who would ever like a day of dieting? Ugh! Have you watched any TV or scrolled the internet lately? We are bombarded with ways to lose weight to shed pounds, feel better, and look great. There is nothing wrong with that if it's healthy and realistic, but that only refers to physical dieting. What if you decided to go on a spiritual diet and cut out the weight of burdens you are carrying or losing inches of excess worry, shedding pounds of discontentment and discouragement, and you start thinking healthy, exercising your body, mind, and spirit? Matthew 11:28-30 (MSG) says: "Are you tired? Worn out? Burned out on religion? Come to me. Get away with me, and you'll recover your life. I'll show you how to take a real rest. Walk with me and work with me—watch how I do it. Learn the unforced rhythms of grace. I won't lay anything heavy or ill-fitting on you. Keep company with me, and you'll learn to live freely and lightly." Can you imagine how much lighter you would be if you gave your burdens over to God? Now, that's a diet with a guarantee! Imagine if you lost worry and gained hope, peace, a smile, and some joy? This would change your life and, inevitably, the lives of those around you. Begin dieting today. Lose all that weighs you down, and Enjoy!

January 6

Good Morning Sunshine! Make it a 'How Do I Love Thee' Day! Think of the people you love, or have loved, throughout your life, those you have given a piece of your heart to. This could be romantic love, friendship, or the love of family. Have you ever given thought to how you love? Are you guarded, or do you love fully? Is your love now, or has it ever been, conditional? Is it based on what others can do for you or how they make you feel? The more they do, the more you love, the better you feel, the better you love. If we are honest, we have all had many conditional love moments. We are blessed to have a God who loves us without condition. We cannot earn it, we cannot escape it, and Jesus said we are to love others just as He loves us. Gulp, what?? We are supposed to love unconditionally too. Does Jesus know the people I know? We want others to love and accept us as we are, but we find it hard to do the same; even with the people we love, forget about our enemies. God is love, God is perfect, and with God, all things are possible, even our ability to love everyone. How do I love thee? Try loving like God. Love all and Enjoy!

January 7

Good Morning Sunshine! Make it a Day of Breaking a Leg. Now, obviously, I don't mean for you to literally break anything but isn't that what we say to people who are about to go on stage and put on a show? Somehow that phrase is meant to offer someone well wishes for a great performance. Well, break a leg, my friends! The only thing is today is not a dress rehearsal, but we do have the opportunity to give today our best shot. We get a chance to live today to the best of our ability and do the best we can. It's too bad that we can't have a dress rehearsal for life, so when we forget our lines, someone is below the center stage to remind us what to say, or when we mess up, we can have the opportunity to try again until we get it right. The only thing we can do is begin our days with a positive attitude and every intention of giving it our best shot, asking for help from those around us when we need it and if we mess up, persevere, try again, knowing that God allows do-overs! Break a leg and Enjoy!

January 8

Good Morning Sunshine! Make it a Day of Accomplishment! You know all the things you meant to finish yesterday, last week, last month, perhaps even last year, but put off until today. We are a culture of procrastinators, always putting things off until the last minute. But isn't it a great feeling when you see your work complete? From one procrastinator to another, I know all too well about this "affliction." The only problem here is that it is self-inflicted. We cause most of our own issues. If we face things as they come or set appropriate priorities, we can accomplish anything before us. Remind yourself that you can do all things through Christ who strengthens you (Philippians 4:13). Set realistic goals and a time frame to complete them. Don't put off 'til tomorrow what you can do today. Face things as they come. Draw strength from God, feel a sense of accomplishment, and Enjoy!

January 9

Good Morning Sunshine! Make it a Day of YOLO! You know, YOLO –You Only Live Once. So, I reflected on that this morning as I looked at a framed picture on my desk that says "This is the beginning of a new day. God has given me this day to use as I will. I can waste it, or I can grow in its light and be of service to others. But what I do with this day is important because I am exchanging a day of my life for it. When tomorrow comes, today will be gone forever. I hope I will not regret the price I paid for it." I realized how true that is. We will never again see this day, we only get one shot at today, and it will be over before we know it, so somehow, we need to make today count for something. We all know that we won't get to do today over, but we don't often think about it in that way or start out with the intent that we better make today worthwhile. My friends, time is flying by, so we can't wait until tomorrow. God has given us this day as a gift. Make today a day that makes an impact, make it significant, let today have meaning and purpose and be a day that makes a difference to you and others around you. You are exchanging a day of your life for it, don't regret the price you paid for today! YOLO – make it count, and Enjoy!

January 10

Good Morning Sunshine! Make it a day of Singing, Dancing, Praising, and Rejoicing! Yes, it's true, people may think you're a little off if you go about your day doing these things. But did you ever notice that we are so much more concerned about what people think of us rather than what God thinks of us. It's true; we think we have to look good, dress perfectly, think like everyone else, and act in a certain way so that others will accept us. We're more people-pleasers than God-pleasers, and it's exhausting, isn't it? We're never going to please everyone. Sorry if that disappoints you, but we can live lives that are pleasing in the sight of God. 1 Thessalonians 2:4 says: "Our purpose is to please God, not people. God alone examines the motives of our hearts." We can choose to live joyfully when others want us to be miserable with them. We can choose to live without fear when others are afraid. We can choose to live freely when others attempt to bind us. So live in a way that pleases God today. If that doesn't make you sing, dance, praise, and rejoice, I don't know what will. Sing, Dance, Praise, Rejoice, please God, and Enjoy!

January 11

Good Morning Sunshine! Make it a Day of Hanging Onto Your Peace! This one, my friends, as I'm sure you know, is easier said than done, but not impossible! We've all had glimpses of God's peace at some point in our lives, some of us for longer periods of time than others. Peace is the assurance that God is with us and knowing that no matter our circumstances, God is in control and all will be well. A wise friend told me once, "All is well, and if all isn't well, all will be well." I had to repeat that a few times to myself to fully grasp the meaning, but her words, to me, were the assurance that with God, I could have peace in spite of my circumstances, challenges, and difficult situations that I found myself in. Although some may deny it, I believe peace is ours if we choose it, yet somehow, we allow our peace to be taken away at the first sign of struggle. We let finances, worry, fear, work, anxieties, stress, relationships, our own haves and have nots, you name it, steal this very precious gift not only out of our hands but out of our hearts, minds, and spirits. Here's the thing...WE LET IT HAPPEN! We allow our peace to be stolen or taken away from us. We allow our peace to be removed, and other life stressors take up residency within us and take over. But here's the beautiful truth, when you trust in God, you know that God has a special purpose for you. When you trust in God, there is a prosperous, bright future for you, not as the world sees it, so stop looking for it that way. Start having a vision and seeing your life through the eyes of Christ! When you know that God is for you, who can be against you? When you know that God loves you, does it matter who or what may not? Peace belongs to you; Jesus said, " Peace I leave with you; my peace I give you. I do not give to you as the world gives. Do not let your hearts be troubled and do not be afraid." (John 14:27). So live today, hanging onto your peace. YOU have the power to do it!! Enjoy!

January 12

Good Morning Sunshine! Make it a Special Day! I know; what is so special about today? Did you ever notice how we wait for the big life moments and milestones to deem the day as special, and rightfully so, but often we miss how special the "ordinary" days are in our lives because we are waiting for the big moments and milestones. Honestly, we don't have time to wait. Today is a special day because this day only comes our way once in a lifetime. Today is special because the possibilities within these 24 hours are limitless. Today is special because you are alive, and you have opportunities to give and receive love. Today is special because you can reach out to help others and make a difference to someone. Today is special because you can feel the wind on your face and the warmth of the sun, because you can choose to work and how to spend your time. Today is special because you can choose to laugh and enjoy life. Today is special if you are in good health and good spirits and able to enjoy the simple pleasures of life. Today is special for so many reasons, and none of them are "ordinary." Embrace the day and if it's not special to you, change that and do all you can to make it special to you and for others! Oh yeah, today's going to be awesome! Enjoy!

January 13

Good Morning Sunshine! Make it a Day of Getting Involved! You may be asking yourself a lot of questions right now, like, how much more involved can I be? What should I get involved in, or why would I want to bother to get involved? All great questions. Involvement doesn't mean doing something on your own but encouraging others to be a part of "something" as well. Don't know what to invest yourself in? Churches, Schools, soup kitchens, hospitals – closer to home, the lives of your family and friends. Why bother? We bother because we were not created for ourselves but for each other. We're given so much, and we're not meant to keep it but to share it! Our purpose is to transform the world by offering hope, extending ourselves for the common good, loving our neighbors as we love ourselves, and living Christ-like. So get involved, invest your hearts & lives, make a difference to someone today and Enjoy!

January 14

Good Morning Sunshine! Make it a Day of Simple Rules! John Wesley, the founder of Methodism, had 3 simple rules; do no harm, do good and stay in love with God. These rules are a piece of cake, aren't they? Don't hurt anyone, please; why would we ever do that? That would mean that we have thought of others as less than ourselves, have ill feelings or harsh words or thoughts toward another, that we have hurt others by our words or actions or that we have treated the world around us with disregard. Oh, right, hmmmm. Now that I think of it, I may have broken this one on occasion. Well, the second rule of doing good is easier anyway. Doing good means helping those in need with my time, talents, gifts, and treasures, with my resources and taking care of my environment, and this may require my commitment, effort, and energy. Hmmm, okay, well, there is a good chance that I haven't always followed this rule as much as I should have either. So far, I'm 0-2. Well, the last rule I know I can follow is simple because I already love God. Oh, wait, except for the times that things were hard and didn't go my way, or when God didn't answer my prayers the way that God should have, or God didn't provide simple solutions and show me the signs I needed. Alright, I admit it... all of these rules sound simple in theory and should be easy to live by, but they're not because often we think that the rules don't always apply to us, yet strangely enough, they apply to everyone else. The truth is that God wants us to follow the rule of loving God, loving our neighbor, and loving ourselves not just because God says so, but because if we do, the simple rules of doing no harm, doing good, and staying in love with God become all the easier to follow and live out. And if we actually followed these rules, imagine the love, joy, and peace we could all live in, not just in our own personal lives, but in the world. Give it your best shot today to follow the simple rules, live blessed lives while blessing others, stay in love with God and Enjoy!

Day | 14

January 15

Good Morning Sunshine! Make it a Day of Being All You Can Be! Nope, not an advertisement for the Army, but what a great message. What if we lived today and every day doing our best and giving it our all? I would often tell my kids, "You don't have to be the best, but you always have to try your best." What good is wasted potential? And, yes, while you have breath, you have potential! Time is going by anyway; you might as well do something about it! How can you be the best you can be? Begin with what God has already given you, the gift of Jesus Christ. Once you recognize the gift, follow His example. Fulfill your potential to love others; trust me, the more you give away, the more love you will have to fill your heart right back up. It might even overflow because there seems to be an endless supply of love returned when you give it away. Live in compassion, generosity, and service, seeing the needs of others and doing all you can to meet those needs. Believe that you can and do make a difference, and then go and live it! Since you only get to live today once, live today, and every day, to its fullest. Fulfill your potential, be all you can be, and Enjoy!

January 16

Good Morning Sunshine! Make it a Day of Anger! That's right, a day of anger! When was the last time anyone gave you permission to be angry? We are often told to suppress our emotions, but where does that get us? It is ok to be angry. Maybe you don't like your circumstances. Currently, not many do. Maybe someone has wronged you, or you just feel like being made because life's not fair; go ahead and do it; get angry! Here's the hard part. Where are you directing your anger? This is where we get into trouble. We often take our anger out on others rather than doing something constructive with it. We need someone to blame, to take the rap because we didn't cause our problems. Sometimes that's true; sometimes it's not. James 1:20 says human anger does not produce the righteousness of God. Ephesians says in your anger, don't sin. We are going to get mad; anger is a part of life, and it is okay to get angry, but use your anger to do something constructive, to change your life or the lives of those in need. Then let your anger go and allow God's peace to reign in your life and Enjoy!

January 17

Good Morning Sunshine! Make it a Day Filled with Blessings! If you woke up this morning, you are blessed. If you have family and friends that love you and you love in return, you are blessed. If you have a roof over your head, food to eat, good health, a mind capable of thinking, and the ability to make choices, then you are blessed! WOW! You may not have even left the house yet, and your day is already filled with blessings. Excellent, the rest of today's blessings should just be icing on the cake! If that is the case, why do we often feel as though our life is unsatisfied or unfulfilled? Why do we overlook the most precious gifts and blessings in search of something more? Sometimes we can't define it; we just know we want more. Open your eyes to your blessings today; your life is full of them. 2 Corinthians 9:8 says: "And God is able to bless you abundantly, so that in all things at all times, having all that you need, you will abound in every good work." God blesses us every day; we just need to open our eyes and our hearts to receive them, embrace them, live into the fullness of them, and thank God for them. You are blessed! Give thanks, be blessed, and Enjoy!

January 18

Good Morning Sunshine! Make it a day of Sweet Dreams! I don't mean rolling over and going back to sleep, although another 15 minutes would have been perfect. When do we wish each other sweet dreams, and why? It's just before we go to sleep, and it could be for many reasons; wishes to rest well and be peaceful, to help our minds focus on the good and let go of everything else, to hope for better things to come. I'm sure you have your own reasons, but the ones I thought of, I could really use today as well, not just tonight before I go to sleep. We all want to have peace, to focus our minds on good and let go of everything else, to hope for better things to come. Why wait until tonight? So, start dreaming, then make all of those things happen today. You can do it! Dream sweet, all day, and make it a rest-full, peace-full, hope-full day and Enjoy!

January 19

Good Morning Sunshine! Make it a Day of Thinking You Can! Sometimes we can draw the greatest wisdom from things we learned as children. Remember the book *"Little Engine That Could?"* That sure feels a lot like life sometimes, doesn't it; carrying heavy loads up the steepest mountains with an engine that is just too tired, too worn down, and full of excuses as to why it can't make it to the top. Life experiences sometimes feel just too burdensome. The challenges we encounter and the struggles we endure, at times, just seem too much to carry. They wear us down. However, if we work hard, if we don't give up, if we stop making excuses for what we can't do and remain optimistic and hopeful in the things we can, truly believing that we can, the seemingly impossible becomes possible. Our impossibilities change to possibilities and become our reality! Scripture tells us in Philippians 4:13: "I can do all things through Christ who strengthens me." Luke 1:37 tells us: "Nothing is impossible with God." Believe it and make it happen! Have faith and hope, and keep moving forward. Don't only think you can; know you can do anything you set your mind and your heart to. Keep your faith in God to help you on your journey, and Enjoy!

January 20

Good Morning Sunshine! Make it a Day of Hearing the Right Voices! We are a funny bunch, aren't we? We are so quick to listen to the opinion of others, but for some reason, we only hear and hang onto the negative. We could have several affirming comments, but one negative statement, word, or even if someone looks at us "the wrong way," we automatically cling to it and make it our own, and it becomes our voice of truth. We have no problem listening to the media when we hear we are not good enough because we don't look a certain way or have certain material possessions. We listen to the voices of judgment from people around us, and we begin to wear those voices like headphones and allow them to play over and over again like a recording on a loop. We are so quick to put ourselves down and allow those voices to resonate within us again and again until we begin to believe them. Why is it easier for us to hear those voices and allow them to dictate who we are rather than holding fast to the voices that tell us that they love us, that we are beautiful, and that we make a difference? If you don't hear someone say any of these affirming words to you out loud, listen more closely, more deeply, to the voice of God, the real voice of truth, the right voice. God loves you! God knows you are beautiful! You are a creation of God; how could you not be beautiful?!?!?! God knows the difference you can and do make in this world! God knows your potential and the possibilities that await you if only you listen to the voice of God. God is telling you in ways that maybe you just have not heard. Zephaniah 3:17 tells us that God is among us, taking great delight in us, and will rejoice over us with singing. The creator of the universe is singing over us...do you hear it???? Listen and hear that voice; the voice of truth, the voice of love, the right voice, and Enjoy!

January 21

Good Morning Sunshine! Make it a Day of Seeing the Sun! Did you look outside yet? Believe it or not, the sun is always shining. Doesn't seem possible when it's been raining, or snowing, or cloudy for days, but you know the sunshine is coming again. You know the feeling when you first see that eek of sunlight. You feel a sense of relief; a smile comes on your face; finally! Life is very much like this. We tend to have long periods of rain, difficulties, struggles, and unpleasant circumstances, and when you get through them, ahhhh, finally! A sense of relief and a smile on your face again. We all know the sun is there and has never left us. We just need to believe it when the storms come. Because of our belief, our hope, our knowledge of the sun and how it doesn't fail us, we can smile and be at peace while we're waiting, through the downpours and the storms. Is it easy, no way! But it is possible and you can make it happen! Carry an umbrella or splash in the puddles; either will help you weather the storm! Read this again, change sun to God; ahhh, finally… Enjoy!

January 22

Good Morning Sunshine! Make it a Day of Realizing Your Potential! Do you ever stop to think about your gifts, talents, and abilities? Do you ever take notice of yourself and the people you have touched in your life, whether you know them or not? You may not even know the people you are affecting with your life, your words, actions, deeds, and with your gifts and talents. You have the potential to change the world. Roy T. Bennett said: "Believe in your infinite potential. Your only limitations are those you set upon yourself." So, start small, one person at a time. Start with you, and recognize how amazing you are. How can you not be? You are created in God's image! You have the potential to do anything you set your heart and mind to. The only thing you have to do is believe it and then live it out. God makes the impossible possible! Your potential and possibilities are endless! Now go change the world! Believe it, live it and Enjoy!

January 23

Good Morning Sunshine! Make it a Day of Following the Leader. I have always loved playing this game. I will still walk like a duck or take super long strides bobbing up and down and hope when I look behind me, someone is there doing the same. I am being silly, but in all seriousness, we first need to determine who or what our leader is before we can begin to follow. Some of us are led by finances (both good and bad). Some of us follow social media or politics, and some of us follow our own desires that lead us in the wrong direction. We should have one leader, the one true example of how to live life in spirit and in truth. That leader is Jesus Christ. When we follow His lead, we live in mercy and compassion, peace and understanding, joy and hope. When that happens, we must then realize that we become leaders who follow in the way that leads to life and when we look back. The hope is that there are others following behind us! Follow Jesus closely. Live by His example. Then lead others to follow you in the right direction, and Enjoy!

January 24

Good Morning Sunshine! Make it a Day of Social Networking. It's what we do anyway, isn't it? We spend so much of our time online, chatting, IM'ing, Zooming, face-timing, texting, and blogging. I'm sure I've missed something, but you get the idea. It's the culture we're in now. Remember when social networking used to be face-to-face interaction? Technology is amazing and has been such a gift and blessing, especially when we are separated by distance, but there is nothing like the real thing; touching, hugging, seeing a smile in person, and having a live conversation. We have been blessed with life and the opportunity to get out and live it to its fullest. God wants us to live an abundant life in relationship with others! Technology certainly helps, but you can't always have relationships behind a computer screen. Go and talk to someone, even if you are socially distanced or wearing a mask. Go and listen to laughter, share stories, and, if possible, give a gentle touch. Be old school and get out today. Be social, really, not virtually, and Enjoy!

January 25

Good Morning Sunshine! Make it a Day of Loving People for Who They Are and Not Who You Want Them to Be! Tough one, right? Why is this so hard? Why can't we love people for who they are? Well, if we get right down to it, it's because we are conditional people. We love those who act in ways that are pleasing to us. We love those who believe what we believe. We love those who look a certain way and speak the way we do. We love those who come from where we come from. We love those who agree with us. We love those who participate in the same things we participate in. We love those who worship the way we worship. And many times, we love those whom we can benefit from while we're profiting from the relationship, of course. Sounds like we use the word "love" a lot, but who are we excluding from our love, and are we actually loving people the way God intended us to love them…for who they really are? Scripture tells us to love God with all of our heart, soul, mind, and strength and to love our neighbor as ourselves. We are never told to pick and choose which neighbors to love but to love them, all of them. This means we are called to love even those who are different than us. God never meant for us to fit the mold of those around us or for anyone to fit our mold or the molds we have created. Much of our struggle with others is because we don't accept or love them for who they are, but rather, we get frustrated for who they are not or who we believe they should be. We live in a world with such amazing diversity of people and cultures; why are we limiting ourselves in loving and embracing all. My hope for each of us today is that we really look at those around us and see everyone as God sees them, as beautiful creations of God. The same God who created you created those different from you. Embrace others for who they are and for who God created them to be and not for who you think they should be. God loves us all the same and accepts us unconditionally. I bet if we start loving everyone, rather than seeking reasons not to love them, our lives will be changed for the better. Try it... I dare you! Open your heart and your life; be accepting and love everyone for who they are, and Enjoy!

January 26

Good Morning Sunshine! Make it a Day of Tuning Out the World and Tuning into God. There is so much noise bombarding us every day, and it gets harder and harder to hear the voice of God. When we listen with our ears, we hear the audible sounds around us. When we listen with our minds, we hear our own thoughts and, more often, the thoughts of others. Our minds then replay the good and bad conversations, stories we have heard on the news or those dreaded infomercials, or even the last song we just heard on the radio that we end up singing all day. However, when we are intentional and listen with our hearts, we hear God no matter what else is going on around us. We hear the voice that offers peace and reminds us not to be afraid because we are not alone. We hear the voice of love that tells us we are beautiful, and we have significance in this world, and that we matter. We hear the voice that offers wisdom, guidance, assurance, and peace that passes all understanding. Tune into God, listen with your heart, and Enjoy!

January 27

Good Morning Sunshine! Make it a Day to Make a Life List! Most make a bucket list of things to do or places to visit before they die. What if you thought about that in a new light, and instead of planning things you want to do before you die, you start making a list of all that you want to accomplish while you're alive! Maybe you're thinking, it's just the same thing said in a different way, but there really is a difference. A bucket list has an ending and is a list of personal achievements. A life list has the same but incorporates so much more, but it never ends. A life list will make you focus on how you're living today, not just on waiting to live until the day you go skydiving, or you buy a new sports car or visit that country you've always wanted to travel to. Rather, it means being alive in this moment, and the next, and the next. How do you want to live today? How can you make the most of it and live today to its fullest? That's truly up to you. My hope is that you're adventurous and live your moments in joy, helping others to do the same. Make your life list today, live it out, add to it again and again, and live it out. Repeat and Enjoy!

January 28

Good Morning Sunshine! Make it a Day of Finding Your Voice! I heard a wonderful commencement speech given by Neil Gaiman; it was brilliant. One statement he made was: "Most only find our own voices after we have sounded like a lot of other people." How many times have you sounded like someone else? There have been many times and occasions that I have tried to emulate, and sound like, others along my journey. I never felt quite good enough, or eloquent enough or educated enough or...whatever it may be, to use my own voice, so I used their voices rather than my own. It never worked out the way I wanted it to. I wasn't comfortable trying to be like, act like or sound like someone else. It wasn't until I had clarity in my heart that I was created uniquely and I was beautifully and wonderfully made for God's glory that I began to discover I had my own voice in this world, and I had better use it for its intended purpose. You too, have a voice, a purpose, and are beautifully and wonderfully made. Sing, shout, speak up, speak out, whisper but find your voice and Enjoy!

January 29

Good Morning Sunshine! Make it a Happy Day! What if we woke up every morning and thought to ourselves, "today, I will choose to live happy and do all that I can to encourage the happiness of others." I don't think I've even thought about this when I wake up in the morning because I usually begin to think about how much more sleep I wish I could have, or I start going over my to-do list in my head. Now I'm not suggesting anyone become a people pleaser by any means, but you don't have to live to please everyone or compromise who you are to foster an attitude of happiness and share that with others. If you make someone smile, let someone know you care, and reach out to help others in need, then you have become a facilitator of happiness. You don't even have to leave your house for this one. Start in your home with the people you live with and then use technology to reach out to those at a distance. Perhaps you can write a letter or send a note or card through the mail. Extend that happiness to the people you work with, travel alongside on the highway, and even people you encounter at a store or restaurant. If you share happiness with just one person each day this week, you will have touched seven lives. In 5 years, that's 1825 lives. You do the math; the potential for sharing happiness is limitless. Be happy, live happy, share happiness, and Enjoy!

January 30

Good Morning Sunshine! Make it a Day of Remembering Those Who Have, Are, and Will Sacrifice on Your Behalf. Think about it; the list is immeasurable. We couldn't possibly begin to realize the enormity of the gift of sacrifice we've been blessed with; the most evident in the life of a Christian is the sacrifice of Jesus Christ that we may live in grace, peace, love & hope, to those who served/serve in the military to ensure our safety and our freedoms to parents who raised us and put us before themselves, to family and friends who sacrifice so much to accommodate for one another. I'm only scratching the surface of the obvious. I encourage you do dig deeper & reflect on those in your life, whether you know them personally or not, who have given of themselves for you. Pray for them, give thanks for them, follow their example, and in turn, ask what it is that you can do for another. Remember, give thanks, give of yourself, share blessings, and Enjoy!

January 31

Good Morning Sunshine! Make it a Full day; a Joy-full, Peace-full, Grace-full, Hope-full, and Faith-full Day! You can experience the most difficult circumstances and be joy-full in spite of challenges and difficulties; let adversity propel you forward and shape your character. The world is chaotic & uncertain; choose to be peace-full within your own heart & spirit. Others may have treated you unfairly, but you can choose to offer grace & forgiveness as God has freely given both to you again & again. Perhaps you don't know how you're going to get through this month, this week, this day, but you can choose to hope & believe that betters times, betters days, and better things are waiting for you. How can you make all these choices to live with a positive outlook and optimistic spirit in spite of it all? Because you have the opportunity to live faith-full lives, to believe in God's promises. If God is for you, who or what can be against you? NOTHING! Have faith, live full and Enjoy!

February

February 1

Good Morning Sunshine! Make it a Seeing with Your Heart Day! My friend, who was blind, once asked me if I knew what the best part of being blind was. I said "no" as I thought to myself, because I didn't think there was a best part of being blind. She then told me the great part was that she was unable to judge people based on their appearance, and she had to get to know someone for who they were and not what they looked like. That was a very profound experience, and from that moment on, I have tried to live blind. Do I always succeed? Nope, but I try. I have met people who appear as though life is fabulous, yet they are falling apart, and others who look a mess yet have it all together. When you take the time to see beneath the surface when you stop seeing with your eyes and start visioning with your heart, you will see the world, humanity, and yourself in a whole new light. You will begin to notice the beauty that has always been around you, and maybe even within you, that you may not have seen. Be blind today so you can truly see and Enjoy!

February 2

Good Morning Sunshine! Make it a day of Ease! We live really complicated lives, don't we? We stress out and worry about everything, especially those things we have no control over. Then, somehow, we begin to take our stress and worry out on the wrong people, usually those closest to us. It comes out in anger, frustration, or sadness. Then we feel bad about it, and we stress out all over again, and the cycle never ends. Well, I want you to know that it doesn't have to be that way. Stressing out and worrying will not change anything, but prayer, surrounding yourself with positive and encouraging people, trusting in God, and being proactive with your life, and your life choices, will. It's not as easy as it sounds, or we would all live stress and worry-free. But it's not impossible. Matthew 19:26 tells us: "With God, all things are possible." We need to believe that, and then we need to live an intentional life of ease, choosing to relinquish control to God. Once the choice is made, our situations may not change, but our stress level will, and we will begin to worry less. Doesn't seem possible, but it's true. Give it a try. Do it! Live in ease, and with ease, today and Enjoy!

February 3

Good Morning Sunshine! Make it a Day of Appreciation! Let's be thankful for everything. Scripture tells us to give thanks in all things, but does God really mean that? If it's raining and it's depressing, and the weather really makes for a bad hair day, how can we be thankful for that? Doesn't God know that life and circumstances aren't always ideal? In fact, sometimes they're terrible, yet we're supposed to give thanks. How is that possible? I have given this thought over many years, and especially in the last several weeks, and I have realized "rain" in life is impossible to escape, though I have tried. I have also come to the understanding that it doesn't last forever. The rain makes me appreciate the sun even more. The hard times make me thankful for the good times. To be fully thankful for my blessings, I have had to hang onto them and remember them in some of life's biggest storms. I have had to see the sun through the rain, and I had to intentionally choose to make something good come from everything. I had to choose to be thankful and appreciate everything! You can choose this too. Choose to see the sun, choose to find goodness, choose to seek out your blessings, and appreciate them all! Give thanks to God, and Enjoy!

February 4

Good Morning Sunshine! Make it a Be Ready for Anything Day! You never know what opportunities or situations may present themselves; let's live prepared. Well, how can we do that if we are not sure what to prepare for? You ask the best questions, awesome! First, if your heart is focused on what is true, what is right, and what is holy, then you are already prepared. You are ready to stand firm and speak up for what you believe in because you know what is true. You are ready to extend a hand to those in need and stand up for social justice and work on behalf of those who are oppressed or marginalized because you know what is right. You are ready to praise God and share the Good News of hope, healing, and wholeness and offer love and grace to all because you know what Holy is. See, you are more prepared than you know. If you have discovered that you are not prepared, it's okay, now, you can start seeking what is true, right, and holy. No one knows everything; that's impossible, yet being ready to say "I don't know, let's find out together" is a good start to being ready for anything. Be ready for anything today! Be ready to love, to help, to use your voice, to be generous, and to give and to learn. Be ready for it all, and Enjoy!

February 5

Good Morning Sunshine! Make it a day of Believing in Yourself! If you don't believe in yourself, in your gifts, talents, and abilities, how can others around you believe in you? You are an awesome creation of God designed intentionally with a meaning and purpose, but it's up to you to discover it and to live it out. There's always a catch, right? Why can't we just be told what our meaning and purpose are? That would make life so much easier, wouldn't it? Not so much. It's actually in the discovery process that we truly begin to understand who we are and where we deepen our relationship with God and others. It's where our convictions and passions are formed and where we become the people God has created us to be. Don't rush the process but glean as much as you can from every experience, every encounter, and every new opportunity you have been given. Be sure to practice patience and believe there is more for your life. Mark 9:23 says, "All things are possible for those that believe." God believes in you. Now it's your turn to believe in the God who created you with meaning and purpose. It's your turn to believe in yourself. Believe and Enjoy!

February 6

Good Morning Sunshine! Make it a day of Saying "I Will!" Our words and thoughts will dictate our days. If we say "I won't," it means we will oppose most anything that comes our way. If we say "I can't," we will inevitably fail before we even begin to try. However, if we say "I will," we can accomplish most anything we set our minds to. Some of our goals take longer to achieve than others, and when we don't get instant results, we become frustrated and have moments where we want to give up. Don't allow that to happen. Continue to say "I will," persevere, and move on toward the goal. You can if you believe you can. You can if you believe that with God, all things are possible. You can if you will. Tell yourself, "I will," and you will be amazed at what you can accomplish. Say it, believe it, do it, and Enjoy!

February 7

Good Morning Sunshine! Make it a Day of Self-Care! How many times do we neglect ourselves and the well-being of our body, mind & spirit? More times than we would like to admit, I'm sure. Yet, if we don't care for ourselves and ensure that our bodies are healthy, well-fed, and well-rested, our minds are sharp and focused, and our spirits are at peace and connected to God, there is no way we can be of any true help or value to those around us? I know, you might ask, aren't we supposed to put God first, others next, and then think of ourselves? The short answer is yes, but we can only do that best when we care for our physical, mental, emotional, and spiritual needs. Take a walk or spend a few minutes resting and re-energizing yourself, meditate or read something for pleasure, spend time laughing or in the company of those who lift you up, sing, dance, be joyful, spend time with God in prayer, study, in nature, through music. Take care of yourself today so that you can fully love God and offer love and care to others and Enjoy!

February 8

Good Morning Sunshine! Make it an O.M.G. day! Now, this is not meant to take the Lord's name in vain but rather to praise God. Do you ever just stop to look at the miracles in your life every day and give thanks to God? Yes, your life is miraculous on so many different levels. The people around you, hard as it may seem sometimes, are also miracles. Have you seen a beautiful sunrise or sunset? O.M.G! miracles very rarely come as trumpets blaring and spotlights shining, and a booming voice announcing its occurrence. They come quietly, simply, and wait for you to notice them. Miracles come in the form of resiliency after struggles, in perseverance in the face of adversity, in the form of strong relationships with family and friends, in our very life and breath, in the creation, and in the hope you have in God, others and yourself. Be aware of the miracles in your life today; they exist. Shout O.M.G. and Enjoy!

February 9

Good Morning Sunshine! Make it a "Trying Something Different Day!" I don't know about you, but every once in a while, I find myself stuck in a rut and bored with the same old routine, so I have to remind myself to break out of it. If I don't like it, whatever "it" is, I should do something about it. John Maxwell said: "You'll never change your life until you change something daily. The secret of your success is found in your daily routine." So today, I encourage you to try something different. Take a different route to work or back home. Go to a restaurant you've never been to or try new food. Get creative; draw, paint, write; you just never know what untapped gifts or talents you may have if you never try. Call a friend or family member you haven't talked to in a long time or invite someone for an impromptu get-together or just take some much-needed time to just be and think or to clear your mind. Just do something out of your ordinary routine today and be blessed in what you may actually discover about yourself in the process! Be different, do different, and Enjoy!

February 10

Good Morning Sunshine! Make it a Day of Praising God Anyway! What if we devoted today to putting God first by seeking guidance, wisdom, and direction from God and praising and worshipping God in all circumstances? Yes, I mean all! If your life is going great, praise God for your blessings! If your life is not going as you would have hoped, praise God for being with you through it. Choose to remember and focus on your blessings throughout your life, the blessings that are difficult to see right now (look harder), and choose to believe in the blessings to come. Choose to rise above it all with the assurance that you are not alone. Praise God, Anyway! You are loved, you are cared for, you are blessed. Live today, and every day, with that understanding. Believe it, acknowledge it, share it, live it. What better example of God's love and faithfulness when you can praise God anyway! Praise God and Enjoy!

February 11

Good Morning Sunshine! Make it a day of Appreciating the Value and Gift of Life. I have seen those who seemingly have nothing appreciate the value and gift of life. I have seen those who have many blessings struggle to recognize all they have and take their gifts and blessings for granted. I have seen those who seemingly have so much working against them, who only have hope and a spirit of determination to only see the good life has to offer, truly value the gift of life. Stop for a moment, take a slow, deep breath and exhale. Give thanks for your life, look for the good in your life, appreciate all you have, and choose to be blessed in this day. I'm not discounting your struggles, but today is happening in spite of us all. If you look for the negative, you will find it. If you seek out joy, you'll find it, probably in the most unlikely of places. Seek joy, take full breaths, see your blessings, appreciate the value and gift of life itself, and Enjoy!

February 12

Good Morning Sunshine! Make it an Inspirational Day! Now, I don't necessarily mean looking for inspiration but more so, being the inspiration. Perhaps it's hard to imagine that you can do this. However, let me persuade you. Do you set goals and work hard to accomplish them? That's inspirational. Do you persevere and cling to your faith even in life's most difficult moments? That's inspirational. Do you laugh and enjoy life or find the most unlikely situations humorous? That's inspirational. Do you practice meekness and refrain from saying harsh words to and about others, when you think or know otherwise? That's inspirational. Have you offered to help those in need without expectation or received help graciously when you were in need? That's inspirational. Kindness, compassion, generosity, joy, hope… they are all inspirational. If you're offering them, you are an inspiration. The truth is, I could go on and on about the many ways you inspire those around you. This is just a reminder to all of us to live being an inspiration. By the way, as you do, you will not only inspire others but you just might also be inspired yourself! Be inspiring, and Enjoy!

February 13

Good Morning Sunshine! Make it a Day of Knowing the Days are Long but the Years are Short. It's funny how fleeting time is. We complain about our long days and our list of things we need to get done in 24 hours, but are we really working to accomplish anything or enjoying life, or are we just trying to get through the day and get it over with? I don't think it's unusual that we, without even knowing it, choose the latter. We can't wait until our workday, our school day, this project, that task, is over. We wish for more time away than we truly live in those moments. We are supposed to do more with today than just get through it. We should be doing more with our lives than just getting through it. We're supposed to live it, cherishing all we've been given while we have it. We're to embrace relationships with friends and family and give thanks for health and love, and opportunities that pass by only once in a lifetime. Nothing lasts forever, the least of which is time. Grab onto life today. Breathe in each moment. Be relevant. Live today on purpose with purpose and meaning. Cherish your time and those with whom you share time. Make your days, every one of them, count. The days are long, but the years are short! Enjoy!

February 14

Good Morning Sunshine! Make it a Day of Recognizing Your One Great Love! To some, this may be your significant other, a family member, pets or friends, an activity like skiing, hiking or traveling, expressing yourself and your passion through creative arts, and to others, it may be as simple as chocolate. It's a gift to love people and things and but if you had to narrow it down, what is your one great love? Don't get me wrong; I love spending time with my family more than anything in the world. I love hearing the sound of their laughter, giving and receiving hugs and breathing them in, and sharing and celebrating life with them. I also love my dog, the sound of the ocean and walking on the beach, trying new foods, and riding my bike, but when I searched my heart, I realized there is more to it; more to life, more to love. All the things I've mentioned are blessings to me, true gifts that I treasure even more because of my one true love; my one great love, Jesus Christ. Because of Jesus, all the things that I love are that much sweeter and more precious. Because of Jesus' love, I have hope, peace, and assurance that I can do all things through Christ who strengthens me; Jesus' love will sustain me! Because of my one great love, all of my other loves are never taken for granted. I have found my one great love, and that love has made all the difference in my life. I hope and pray that your one great love will do the same. Search your heart today and find and embrace your one great love and Enjoy!

February 15

Good Morning Sunshine! Make it a Day of Taking One Step at a Time. We often have so many thoughts running through our minds at once, don't we? I have to do this, be here, meet with so and so, finish this so I can start that. By the time we are done thinking about it, we are overwhelmed and exhausted. Does this sound familiar? We live hectic lives with crazy schedules and agendas, thinking we can multi-task and accomplish it all at once. Sometimes we luck out, and that happens. Most of the time, we are stressed out and anxious. The theologian, Martin Luther, said: "I am so busy that I shall spend the first three hours in prayer." While that may not be realistic, there are other things we can do. First, take a deep breath and exhale slowly. Now start over. Prayer may not be a bad way to start. Then, prioritize your day, focusing on ONE thing at a time. Complete one task before you take on another. You will work more efficiently and with better results. You may actually enjoy meeting with so and so or working on a project because you are not consumed with thoughts of your next activity. Be focused, be intentional, pray and breathe in the Spirit of God, exhale everything else and accomplish everything one step at a time and Enjoy!

February 16

Good Morning Sunshine! Make it a Day of Embrace. Did you ever try to hug someone while running? Have you attempted to enjoy a sunrise or sunset in 30 seconds or less? Did you ever have a significant or meaningful conversation as fast as possible? Have you figured out the direction your life is headed or made serious decisions in a matter of seconds? Of course not, nor should you. Life, relationships, people, nature, living with meaning and purpose, struggle, choices, and decisions are all meant to be embraced and not to be done in haste. Don't rush life; embrace it. Don't take for granted relationships and people; embrace them and value them, every time you can. Stop and watch a sunset, wake up early to see the sunrise, and embrace the beauty of nature around you. Embrace opportunities to pray and spend time with God. Embrace your struggles. While not easy to embrace, it is necessary. We learn who we are in the face of adversity. Live significantly. You can and should live with meaning and purpose because you have meaning and purpose. Embrace that. Take it ALL in today; live, embrace and Enjoy!

February 17

Good Morning Sunshine! Make it a Brave Day! That is not always easy when the world is a frightening place. Have you watched the news? Scary stuff. Sometimes our fears can feel overwhelming. However, scripture tells us to be courageous, to have no fear because God is with us wherever we go. If we know that in our minds and believe it in our hearts, then nothing should ever stand in our way of accomplishing whatever it is that we set out to do, and there will be no fear preventing us from moving forward in life. We will be able to accomplish whatever God has called us to do. Okay, so how come that doesn't always happen? Well, sometimes, there is a disconnect between our knowing and our believing. We can know something in our minds and believe something in our hearts, but until the two connect (heart & mind), we may allow fears to hinder our journey. If we only follow our minds, we can rationalize anything and allow fears to stop us from moving forward. If we only use our hearts, we may not use logic, and we might operate on pure emotion, and fears will stop us dead in our tracks. However, when we use our heart and mind together, along with our faith, we are blessed with courage and love that comes from God, and things become we never knew to be possible become possible, in spite of our fears. Being brave doesn't always mean not being afraid; most often, it means moving forward, trying something new, overcoming obstacles, or taking a risk while being afraid. When you know in your heart and mind that God is with you, you can choose to live in courage. Choose to live brave today, and don't let anything stop you and Enjoy!

February 18

Good Morning Sunshine! Make it a Day of Being and Doing. What does this mean? How do you "be" and "do?" As someone of faith, I believe it means to be the person God has created you to be and do what you need to do in order to live that out. How does this get accomplished? First, you need to know who you are before you can truly be you. What kind of person are you? What is your character? What roles do you have? Are you a parent, student, friend, leader, worker, or volunteer? What things do you enjoy doing? Do you enjoy painting, singing, cooking, playing or watching sports, or helping others? Once you determine who you are, then you need to choose to do something about it, to live it out. By the way, who you are, changes over time because you are not who you were years ago or even yesterday, and this may take more than a day, don't rush the discovery process, but start now! You are a unique and beautiful creation designed with the ability to be and do anything. How awesome is that? Don't waste a single opportunity to live out your life to its fullest. Be you and do all that you can to fulfill your purpose. Be, do and Enjoy!

February 19

Good Morning Sunshine! Make it a Day of Casting Your Burdens! We carry so many worries, anxieties, concerns, and burdens; call them what you want to, but we are weighed down with so much every day when we don't have to be. Did you ever see someone who is happy all the time? Our thoughts about them are usually one of two things; first, they are annoying and living in denial, or I really wish I could be like them and be happy too. No one lives a perfect life, and so many of us endure difficult circumstances, yet, some choose not to worry and rise above it all and live happy. Let me let you in on a secret...You can be that person! We are told to give it all to God; give our burdens, worries, fears, and anxieties, but we don't. 1 Peter 5:7 tell us to cast our burdens unto Jesus because He cares for us. In Matthew 6, We are also told that not a minute of worry will add time to our lives, yet we worry. If you have faith, if you trust God, then you only need to pray, give everything to God and lose the extra weight of worry or struggle. Best diet plan I know of! Your circumstances might not change, but you and your outlook and peace of mind will. Cast your burdens, annoy, or perhaps even be contagious to others with happiness and Enjoy!!!

February 20

Good Morning Sunshine! Let's make it a day for moving, moving on, moving up, moving ahead, moving forward, moving in any direction except backward! We are a people of God transforming from glory to glory, changing and growing daily. We are a people created by God with the purpose of moving the kingdom of God forward and to do all we can to get others wrapped up in our movement along the way. Let go of the way it used to be, and remember what you have gained from experience. Don't look back on what was unless it is to help propel you forward. So many people look back and get stuck there. Use what you have learned and look ahead and move toward the beauty of what can, will, and should be! Jeremiah 29:11 says: "For I know the plans I have for you," says the Lord. "They are plans for good and not for disaster, to give you a future and a hope." As a people of God, we are to have hope, and we are called to move hope forward because we trust in God's promises. God has a great plan for your future, but you need to see with the eyes of God, trust in God's holy word, and move with the hope of God in order for the plan to unfold. So, what are you waiting for? Get moving and Enjoy!

February 21

Good Morning Sunshine! Make it a Day of Being Honest with Yourself. Have you ever asked yourself some tough questions about where you are in life now or what choices you made to arrive here? Do you like where you are, or do you need to make changes? Have you asked yourself where is it that you want to go and what is it that you want to accomplish, and how will you make it happen? Have you focused on your relationships, those that are close, and those relationships that have their struggles? What makes them successful or causes strain? Perhaps this should have been a day of questioning rather than a day of honesty, but first, questions need to be raised so you can answer honestly. The truth is no one in the world will know the answers but you, and God, so you have nothing to lose by being honest with yourself, but you do have everything to gain. Can there be some wrong answers here? Yes, so think before you answer. Take time for reflection, to learn about yourself. Once you have the answers, nothing will stop you from moving forward and living fully. Share you, with you, honestly, and Enjoy!

February 22

Good Morning Sunshine! Make it a day of seeing things in a different light. We have become so used to our surroundings, our homes or workplace, nature and the environment around us, even the people we associate with, our family and friends, that we forget to really see everything as we should. Life, our routines, our interactions become rote, mundane, you know, the same old same old. Shed new light on everything today and look as if you are seeing things for the first time. When it comes to relationships, try to see the world through the eyes of others, even if only for a moment. You will see differently and notice things that you never saw before, even though they were right before you the whole time. If you look closely, you may even see God at work, changing and transforming the world around you. Better yet, light may be shed on you, your life, and God at work in you, through you, and even in spite of you. In John 8:12, Jesus tells us: "I am the light of the world. Whoever follows me will never walk in darkness but will have the light of life." Maybe if we begin to see things, and people, through the eyes of Christ, we will have no choice but to see things in a different light. Look for the brightness; it's there. See the light today in the world, in others and in you, and Enjoy!

February 23

Good Morning Sunshine! Let's make it a day of Getting Back in the Loop! Often life's circumstances, whether good or bad, can throw us off track and take us places we could never have imagined. No matter where we are physically, God wants our hearts, minds, and spirits to be centered and focused, to be in the loop, so to speak, with the love, peace, and joy of God. Philippians 4:8-10 tells us how to "stay in the loop: "And now, dear brothers and sisters, one final thing. Fix your thoughts on what is true, and honorable, and right, and pure, and lovely, and admirable. Think about things that are excellent and worthy of praise. Keep putting into practice all you learned and received from me—everything you heard from me and saw me doing. Then the God of peace will be with you." So, if you are out of the loop, pray and seek support from God and others to get back on track. If you are in the loop, pray, provide support and encouragement for those in need, and continue to seek support from others to stay on track. Either way, pray and keep strong connections with God and people to give and receive encouragement and support. Be in the loop, and Enjoy!

February 24

Good Morning Sunshine! Make it a Day of Singings God's Praises. Maybe you woke up on the "right" side of the bed this morning, and circumstances are good, or just status quo and praising God seems natural and easy. Great, share God's goodness and let those around you know how God blesses you. But what if your side of the bed always seems to be the wrong one to get out of? Does this provide a get-out of praising God-free card? On the contrary, it calls for us to praise God even more and to let others know how God blesses us in spite of everything. We see the struggle as bad rather than seeing God in the midst of it. Faith, hope, and trust in God and our own character, humility, resiliency, and perseverance are defined in adversity. Praise is a response to God's gracious invitation to lift our eyes to Jesus, our Savior, despite our feelings or circumstances. We are to praise God anyway, in all ways, and give thanks in all circumstances, yes, all! Why? Because no matter what, God is with us, and this calls for our praise! Praise God and Enjoy!

February 25

Good Morning Sunshine! Make it a Day of Recalling Good Memories. You know what I mean when you are with family and friends, and someone says: "remember when..." and suddenly the stories begin, followed by laughter and the joy of times spent together. Now, this is not to look backward to get stuck there but more as a reminder of where we have been and how there have been good and wonderful people who have blessed our lives. Think of those who have come and gone and somehow have enriched your life and helped you grow along your journey to help shape you to become the person you are today. As you remember, give thanks. Thank God for the gift of love and joy, laughter and friendship of family and fellowship, and for allowing you to remember, hang onto and cherish memories of those who have blessed your life for the better. Remember the good times and the beautiful people, using both to help you create more good memories with others. Remember and Enjoy!

February 26

Good Morning Sunshine! Make it a Day of Trust! Trust isn't something that comes easily, especially in today's world, but it is an essential quality of our closest and deepest relationships. Is there anyone who feels as though they haven't been "burned" before because they put their trust in someone only to be let down and feel betrayed? We have all been there. Perhaps we have been on both sides as well, the disappointed and the disappointer. Either way, we have got to try again. Gain wisdom from disappointments and trust in yourself and your instincts. Trust in those who love and care about you. Trust in new relationships. And more than anything, trust in God. Proverbs 3:5-6 says: "Trust in the Lord with all your heart and lean not on your own understanding. Acknowledge him in all your ways, and he shall direct your path." If you want God to lead you, trust. If you need to make decisions, pray and trust. If you feel lost or lonely, humble yourself, be patient, and trust that God has a plan for you. Trust and Enjoy!

February 27

Good Morning Sunshine! Make it a Day of Being Nice and Sharing Kindness! Seems easy enough, that is until our feet hit the floor and we realize we are running late, or we spill the coffee, or we get stuck in traffic, or that person cuts us off. How we treat others is often dependent on how we feel. If we are in a good mood, the people around us luck out because there is a good chance we will share a smile or a kind word, but if we are not happy, then brace yourself world, because you are getting nothing from me! How we treat others cannot, and should not, be dictated by our own circumstances and emotions, yet that happens far too often. Jesus is an example of how not to do this. If he was tired, frustrated, or just wanted to be alone, he still treated people with compassion, offered love, mercy, and kindness, and spoke words of hope. This was not based on his own emotions, but it was the right thing to do. It was, and is, the Godly thing to do. We are to follow the example of Jesus and do the same! Smile, be nice, express joy and hope, and share kindness with others. Do these things, and it will help others, and they just might change you! Enjoy!

February 28

Good Morning Sunshine! Make it a Colorful Day! The world wants us to see in black and white, and often, that's how our minds think; black and white, cut and dry, the matter of fact, and it is so limiting. That's great sometimes, but not every person or situation fits into our mold, and not everyone's life fits into our color pallet. The world around us is vibrant, and the people around us are diverse on every level. God doesn't think in terms of black and white, cut and dry and matter of fact, or in limitations. If so, where would Grace come into play? Luckily, we don't have to be concerned because God has created each one of us uniquely with meaning and purpose to live brilliant, colorful, vibrant lives. We just need to stop limiting our thoughts and the way we see people and the world and begin seeing the beautiful colors around us. We need to be more open to what's directly in front of us, loving others for who they are and experiencing all that God and life has to offer. Live colorfully and Enjoy!

February 29

Good Morning Sunshine! Make it a day of Having Faith. Scripture tells us if we have faith, even as small as a mustard seed, we can move mountains, and nothing would be impossible. I have been told that faith will move mountains, but you better bring a shovel. Wait a minute; that means we have to put in some effort? Can't we just pray and make things happen? Yes, it's true. Having faith is a verb, meaning it requires some action, and faith without action is dead. You cannot just will something to happen or pray for it to happen without being willing to do your part to make it happen. If you have faith and believe with your heart, then you will be prompted to work toward fulfilling your goals and allowing God to use you to make things happen. Pray, believe, and be prepared. All things are possible with God and your willing heart, spirit, and determination. Have faith and Enjoy!

March

March 1

Good Morning Sunshine! Make it a Day of Praying on Behalf of Others. We all know so many people who are going through difficult times, experiencing health, relationship, personal and/or emotional and financial struggles. We see this on every human level. We see this as a nation. We see it in our world. There are many around us who have lost hope. Life is hard, and we are all faced with challenges at some point. There's no doubt about it, but life isn't hopeless. Pray for those around you today. You don't need to know the details to know that everyone you encounter is struggling or is close to someone who is going through difficult times. Pray for them. There is no greater gift that you can provide than lifting someone up to God in prayer. 1 Timothy 2:1 says: "I urge you, first of all, to pray for all people. Ask God to help them; intercede on their behalf and give thanks for them." Seize the opportunity to come before God, trusting, believing, and hoping for others to feel the healing presence of God in their lives. Give thanks, have hope, pray and Enjoy! P.s. you have been prayed for today!

March 2

Good Morning Sunshine! Make it a Day of Practicing! Doesn't practice make perfect? Well, what if we practice everything we do until we get it right? To learn how to laugh, be positive and joyful, practice laughing and seeking the good in every situation, every person, and every experience. It might take practice, but the good will be there if you look for it. To learn how to dance, forget about those who watch and practice dancing! To learn how to give, be generous, and practice giving! To learn how to forgive, let go of grudges, and practice forgiveness. To learn how to love, open your heart, and practice loving! To learn how to serve, give your time and energy to others and practice serving! To learn how to live, let go of fears, and practice living! It is true; I could go on and on because we perfect those things we practice. Scripture tells us in Philippians 4:9: "What you have learned and received and heard and seen in me—practice these things, and the God of peace will be with you." Practice whatever it is that you need to perfect today. If we begin to look at all we do as a practice, when we make a mistake, it will be much easier to get up and try again rather than think we can't do something. Practice makes perfect; all you have to do is try, and most likely, try again! Practice and Enjoy!

March 3

Good Morning Sunshine! Make it a Day of Traveling! Get in your car, catch a flight…ok, that would be nice, but it's not the type of traveling I'm referring to. This isn't about getting away; it's about getting within; destination-YOU! We all need to take a journey within the heart, mind, and soul every so often, and it's not a place that you can escape from, although many have tried. Molly Kate Brown said: "The single most sacred pilgrimage you will ever make is the one right where you are." Several times in our lives, we need to reflect on where we have been, where we are currently, and where we are going. The first two may be uncomfortable to visit but easier than determining where we are going next. The journey of life isn't always easy and without challenges and obstacles, but there are many blessings along the way if you choose to take the time to see them as you're passing by. When obstacles change our course of direction or if we are traveling too fast, we often allow ourselves to miss the goodness and the blessings on our journey. Take the time to journey within today. Where are you going? You may find there is no better place to be than with you! Get going and Enjoy!

March 4

Good Morning Sunshine! Make it a day of Asking, Seeking, and Knocking! I hope you had a beautiful weekend and you are ready to embrace all this week has in store for you. If your week is already full and you haven't left the house yet on Monday morning, how about letting go of embracing what this week has in store for you and instead, embracing all that God has in store for you. Scripture tells us to ask and receive, to seek and find, to knock, and doors will be opened. We just need to remember to ask for the right things, blessings of peace, love, patience, strength, courage, endurance, healing, or whatever it is that you are in need of today, and then ask God to provide for your needs. Take the time to listen, to seek God's guidance and direction, and really look and listen, not only with your eyes but with your heart. You will be amazed at the blessings that are right before you and the opportunities to knock on the right doors. We are always knocking in the wrong places or the same doors over and over again, expecting to be blessed. This is where that seeking guidance thing comes in handy! Blessings are waiting for you. Ask, seek, knock, and you will find! Enjoy!

March 5

Good Morning Sunshine! Make it a Day of Reclaiming Your Territory. I once had a new deck put on my house, and I was saddened when the beautiful vine wrapped around the previous deck was removed in the process. In the days and weeks that followed, I noticed that the vines had a triumphant return and began to take their place, wrapping around the spindles once again. I have also noticed as I drive along the highway that the barriers created to separate neighborhoods from the roadway and the noise that comes with it have also begun to be taken over by nature once again. In some areas, you can barely notice the barrier because of the vines and greenery. It's amazing; Nature is reclaiming its territory. Wouldn't it be great if we could do the same? Is there a part of you that you feel has been lost, removed, or torn down in the process of life and circumstances? My deck vine returned even though it was torn apart and seemingly destroyed. It came back newer, greener, and stronger because the root, its source of life, and strength were still there. You can do the same and take back those parts of you, and your life that you believe are missing. How? The root, God, your source of life and strength, is still with you. Reclaim you today. Reclaim God in your life today and become newer, stronger, and better than ever. Believe it, reclaim it and Enjoy!

March 6

Good Morning Sunshine! Make it a Day of List Making! Really, couldn't you come up with something better than list-making? What kind of day is this? We could call it a day of counting our blessings, but we would forget to count them and forget our blessings. Well, today, keep your paper and pen handy and every time you think of a blessing, write it down. I'll get you started. First, you woke up this morning. Second, someone has already prayed for you (I did). Your turn, go! Why? What's the purpose? Sometimes we need visual reminders of how we are blessed because we take so much in our lives for granted. Sometimes life is just hard, and we need to be reminded that there really are good things in our lives, that we are not alone, and that someone cares for us when we can't or don't feel it. Sometimes something as goofy as a list right in front of us will remind us. Cumbersome, slightly annoying? Sure it is. But make a list anyway. Then read it, commit it to memory, believe it, and live as blessed people! Enjoy!

March 7

Good Morning Sunshine! Make it a Day of Jumping to Conclusions! We do this, don't we? When reading a book, we skip to the last page before we finish the first chapter. We want to know the ending before we have barely begun. We need to be assured the main characters are okay. Well, we do this with our own lives, too, and we are the main characters. We want to know the end before we go through all the chapters, so we jump to conclusions and create scenarios of how things should be for us and for others, only we often conclude the worst and rarely hope for the best. What if, instead of jumping to the worst conclusions, we just jumped to much better conclusions like we are loved, cared for, never alone, we can accomplish anything, and those who love us will support and encourage us. Do we ever jump to these conclusions? No, quite the opposite. If we did, we actually wouldn't need to jump to any conclusions or need to know the end because we would live in confidence, self-worth, trust, hope, and faith. If you have to, jump to the best conclusions, take your time, read each chapter of your life, find assurance in God and Enjoy!

March 8

Good Morning Sunshine! Make it a day of Too Much! We often think we don't have enough, especially when we see others who seem to "have it all." How did they luck out? They have the biggest houses, the nicest cars, the best wardrobe, etc. They have more than we do; they have too much stuff. Well, "they" may have stuff, but that shouldn't be our focus. Honestly, we all have too much, and we could share if we wanted. We possess too much within us to keep it to ourselves, but we do. We all have too much love, too much generosity, too much hope, too much kindness, too much faith. We have too much, but for some reason, we think we are lacking, so we hang onto it, all of it! You have it all, don't be afraid to give too much away. Let me share a secret, it's really only yours if you use it, and you will find that if you give away too much of what you have, your love, kindness, compassion, hope, etc.., you are going to get too much of the same in return! Let it go, give too much away, get too much back! It's a beautiful cycle! Enjoy!

March 9

Good Morning Sunshine! Make it a Day of Giving It Away! What is it? Well, I'm not talking about material things and giving away all of your personal belongings, but I am talking about something very personal. 'It' is YOU! We are a people who like to hang onto everything we have for fear if we give it away, we will be left with nothing. However, I believe otherwise. When you give away smiles, more than likely, they will be returned to you. When you give away friendship, joy, love, compassion, and kindness, they often come back tenfold. Now, I'm not saying give it away so you see what you can get. I'm suggesting to give these things away because it is the right thing to do; it's the God thing to do. We have been given so much, and we are truly blessed with gifts that money can't buy, not to keep, but to give away, all of it! Don't hang onto anything; give it, give love, give joy, give peace, give hope, give God, give YOU, give now and Enjoy!

March 10

Good Morning Sunshine! Make it a Day of Being Slow to Speak and Quick to Listen. Often our natural instinct is to respond to someone before we have had time to process what has been said, especially when tempers are flaring or our excitement level is high. We are always thinking of our response, and we are just waiting for others to finish so that we can talk. Many times, we start speaking before they are even done. It happens to all of us. We want to get our point across, we want to be heard, and we want to get in the last word. Deeper than that, we all want to be validated and know what we say means something to someone. By the way, speaking louder doesn't mean others will hear you. It may be just the opposite. The Dalai Lama said: "When you talk, you are only repeating what you already know, but if you listen, you may learn something new." Be a good listener today. Give others your undivided attention. Validate them and hear what they are saying, whether you like it or not. You never know what you will hear. If there is an opportunity for response, think first, speak slowly, in love and kindness. Be slow to speak and quick to listen, and Enjoy!

March 11

Good Morning Sunshine! Make it a Day to Give Up! Huh? I know, perhaps not the greeting you were expecting, but as usual, there's a method to my madness! Believe it or not, this is a positive message because I don't mean throw your hands up, retreat or cave in. On the contrary, I'm asking you to give up all those things that can potentially cause you to stop moving forward! Give up thinking today isn't going to be an amazing day, make it amazing! Give up thoughts that tell you that you're not good enough, smart enough and start believing that YOU are enough! You're created by God in the image of God, how could you not be enough? Give up complaining about people and circumstances. If you don't like it, change it, and become part of the solution rather than compounding the problem! Give up thinking you can't and tell yourself YOU can do all things through Christ who strengthens you! Give up not standing up for yourself or others in need and with all that you have and all that you are, use your gifts, talents, resources to help others. Give up silence and use your voice to share words of love, compassion, joy, hope, kindness, and to share the Good News! Give up your fears and live in the moment, life's too short not to. For God's sake, give up your need for control and let God take over! What a difference that will make, I promise! Give Up and Enjoy!

March 12

Good Morning Sunshine! Make it a Better Day Than Yesterday. Today is a new day; we all get a fresh start and have the opportunity to make it better than yesterday. Choose to see the good in everything and everyone and see the good in you today. Take time to connect with family and friends, time to be with God, and time to be with you. Seek out the beauty in creation, the beauty in others, and the beauty in you. Take deep breaths and take in the goodness and blessings that are in your life. Breathe in God. Exhale slowly and let go of everything else, stress, anxieties, and worries. Look for God all around you, in nature, in others, in you! No matter how your day was yesterday, good, bad, or indifferent, make today better. You have the ability to do so; how awesome is that!?! You get to call the shots. Perhaps you don't get to choose the situations or circumstances you are in, but you get to determine your response and to find good, see good, do good and make today and your attitude better than yesterday! It's your choice; choose wisely! Make it the best day ever, until tomorrow and Enjoy!!

March 13

Good Morning Sunshine! Make it a Day of Promoting Peace. If you watch the news, spend time on social media, listen to the radio or read the newspapers, you see that the world around us is anything but peaceful. It's hard for us to live in peace when we, our friends or our family members, and innocent people around the world are experiencing unsettling, painful, and unfathomable circumstances. How can we promote peace when life is chaotic? It may not be easy, but peace must begin within us in order for us to promote peace and live it out. It's challenging, to say the least when external forces are so influential to our peace of mind. We are reminded in scripture that all of these troubling things and events that we read and hear about are going to happen, but as followers of God, we are supposed to live in peace, free from fear. Why? It's not because the circumstances aren't frightening, because they really are, but because we have knowledge that we are not on our own. We know that God is with us and has not left us alone in this world. When we believe that we are not alone, we gather strength; we become less fearful, and we gain a sense of calmness and a sense of security. We then live more fully. Just with this knowledge and belief, we gain a sense of peace, and we are given opportunities to promote peace. Find peace within you and in your faith in God. Live in peace and do all you can to promote peace and Enjoy!

March 14

Good Morning Sunshine! Make it a day of the Positive Spin!! We have all heard the saying, "Life is what you make it," and that can be true. If we have a negative outlook, chances are things in our life may go in a negative direction, or we will think it is. However, if we put a positive spin on things and seek out the good in every situation, chances are, positivity and goodness will come our way, or at least we will think they will. I am not suggesting we have a "Pollyanna" outlook on life. We do need to think rationally. Yet, I do believe that we will find what we are looking for, good or bad. Wouldn't you rather find the good? Life will throw a lot at us; it is up to us to put a positive spin on it. God has blessed us with so much, creation, family, friends, life, breath, opportunity, faith, love, peace, joy, and hope. Don't you just love long lists, especially when they are filled with good things? Me too! God gave us Jesus, who came to give us life, abundant life. Wow! All these blessings in abundance! Now that puts a positive spin on everything! Let's spin positively today and Enjoy!

March 15

Good Morning Sunshine! Make it a Day of Believing in You! We believe in the craziest of things, don't we? We believe if we wish upon a star, see the clock at 11:11, or blow out birthday candles, our wishes will come true. We believe much of what we see in print, watch on television, or read on the internet, but how often do we take the time to believe in ourselves? How regularly do we believe we are so much more? How many times have we believed we could overcome all the odds and do anything that we set our mind to? How often do we feel something in our hearts and know it in our minds but allow words, doubts, fears, or even beliefs of others to make us believe otherwise? Today is the day to challenge all of that and believe in you and the person God created you to be! You are beautifully and wonderfully made to accomplish so much in this life, more than you know, more than others know, but exactly what God knows! Believe it! Believe in yourself and live like you do, and Enjoy!

March 16

Good Morning Sunshine! Make it a Day of Trying Again! If at first, you don't succeed, try, try again. Yeah, yeah, blah, blah, blah. I know it is hard to keep trying when it seems as though you are giving it all you've got, and it doesn't seem to be working or quite enough; I get it; we have all been there. Maybe you are there now. It takes tremendous courage to keep trying when burdens weigh you down, and life is tough, and you seem to be traveling uphill. It sure would be nice to be on a flat road or even a slight downhill once in a while, wouldn't it? Well, I can't tell you that will happen, but I can remind you that you are not alone in your journey. God has been, is, and will always be with you. All you have to do is recognize God's presence, believe God is with you, and have the hope and the courage to keep trying. 2 Chronicles 15:7 says: "But as for you, be brave and don't lose heart, because your work will be rewarded!" We often believe if we don't see it, we can't believe it, and if you can't believe it, you can't hope for it. So, here is your reminder to open your eyes, breathe in God's Spirit and God's goodness and then exhale everything else and try again! Try it now, and if necessary, try it again and Enjoy!!

March 17

Good Morning Sunshine! Make it a Day of Beginning at the End! Today is St. Patrick's Day, and many people are looking for that "Pot of Gold." But you can't begin a journey without having a destination in mind. If you know where you are headed, you can make plans and prepare. We all want to be lucky, to get rich quickly, have our goals met immediately, and take the easy way out whenever possible, but rarely do such things happen. The truth is, if you know what you want in life and where you want to go, and the goals you'd like to accomplish, you'll have to start the journey, take a step forward and work toward them. But you need to have a goal in mind and "see the end of the rainbow" in your heart before you begin the trip. So where is it you're going today? What is it that you'd like to accomplish in the next 24 hours? If you begin knowing the goals you'd like to achieve, then you'll prepare and do all you can to make them happen. In essence, you'll have a destination in mind and start navigating toward it. On a bigger scale, what are the goals you have for your life? What do you need to begin today to prepare for bigger goals or larger accomplishments that you'd like to achieve during your lifetime? Begin at the end, and have a vision in mind. Know where you're headed, put the effort in to arrive at your destination, and embrace the journey along the way. It will take a little more than luck to get you there, but never stop searching, and working toward, that Pot of Gold at the end! Enjoy!

March 18

Good Morning Sunshine! Make it a Day of Following the Golden Rule! Easy enough, right? Treat others as you want to be treated. Piece of cake! Let's tell that to our kids when they won't get up in the morning, to the guy who cut you off on the highway, to your boss who keeps adding to your work pile, or to the cashier who needs a price check on something delaying your purchase and return home. It's easier to say we will treat others how we want to be treated than to actually live it out. It's much simpler to treat others how we want to be treated when things go our way. You may refrain from harsh words, but what is your facial expression? Do you roll your eyes when frustrated, sigh loudly for all to hear, or throw your hands up and walk away? Yeah, me too. God meant it when we were told to love our neighbor and our enemies, not just when it's convenient for us or if others are nice to us, but always! This is an "always" kind of rule! How do you want to be treated today? Do you want to be treated with kindness, love, compassion, generosity, sincerity... great! Go treat others this way first, and Enjoy!

March 19

Good Morning Sunshine! Make it a day of Quitting Your Complaining! The truth is, we are big complainers. We can be so whiney, and we complain about everything, don't we? If we don't have anything to complain about, we look for things to complain about. We, as a culture and society, complain about everything from politics to religion to the weather being too hot or too cold. We complain about family and friends or complete strangers who annoy us: "omg, can you believe they are wearing that, loving him or her, spending money on this, working there, living the way they do, or not doing things the way we would do them?" You can add your own complaint here. If we put half as much energy into letting people live the way they choose, wearing or loving whatever or whomever they want, or if we spent time solving our own problems or trying to change things that bother us, then the world, or at least our small portion of it, would be much more peaceful. Matthew 7:3 says: "And why worry about a speck in your friend's eye when you have a log in your own?" We only get one life to live. Do we want to embrace it and enjoy it or whine and complain about it? Either way, the choice is yours. My suggestion, change whatever it is you're complaining about or adjust your attitude. Quit your complaining and seek out some goodness in your life. You will always find what you look for. Stop complaining, live happy and in peace and Enjoy!

March 20

Good Morning Sunshine! Make it a Day of Knowing You Are Loved! Many go through life not really sure that they are liked, let alone loved. The world is judgmental, and we allow those judgments to distort our view of ourselves, and we begin to base our ability to be loved and cared for and our value, on the external. We base so much on physical appearance or material possessions and wealth. We discount the internal, our hearts, character, integrity, and our gifts and talents because we are busy comparing ours with others we deem as being better than us. In turn, we never fully embrace or use all that we have been blessed with. 1 John 4:16 says: "God is Love." If we have been created in God's own image, and God is love, well, it must mean that we are love too. If we have been created in love and we are love, then we must be loved! God loves us, no matter the world's opinion. 1 John 3:1 tells us: "See how very much our Father loves us, for he calls us his children, and that is what we are!" Friends, if you are a child of God, YOU ARE LOVED! You need to know that you are loved by God. If you know it and believe it, then you will live it and share it! YOU ARE LOVED, and there is nothing you can do about it except embrace it! So embrace the knowledge that you are loved. Know it, live it, share it, and Enjoy!

March 21

Good Morning Sunshine! Make it a Day of Living in Faith, Not Fear! In the news, we hear of terrible events that result in tragedy and loss of innocent lives, the pandemic and its variants, political unrest, and nations divided. We hear of terrorist attacks and natural disasters. We are bombarded with fear. Closer to home, we have difficult relationships, unemployment, financial burdens, and failing health. When you look at the world like this, who wouldn't be afraid? There is seemingly so much to be afraid of on the surface, but our faith can be stronger than our fears. Does this mean we'll never be afraid? I'm sorry to say; it doesn't. What it does mean is that our faith can help us cope with our fears. Our faith can help us overcome our fears. Our faith can help us move forward in spite of our fears. Faith in God means believing in God's promises that God will never leave us nor forsake us. Does this mean we won't have hard times? I wish, but no, it doesn't mean that either. What it means is that there is hope for better days, better times, better lives, and peace, not as the world knows it, but from within, as God knows it. We can combat our fears because we know that we are not alone; God is with us through it all. You can choose to live in peace because you know that you are not alone! You cannot fully live and embrace life, experience new things, love, share, and be, if you allow fear to overtake you. Be wise in the world, but live in faith, believe in God's promises, hold onto hope and Enjoy!

March 22

Good Morning Sunshine! Make it a Worthwhile day! We are going through the day anyway, right? Well, our options to make it meaningful and rewarding are limitless. Psalm 90:12 says: "Teach us the brevity of life so that we may grow in wisdom." Wisdom should tell us to make the most of our days, time is fleeting, and we need to live with relevancy and to make every day worthwhile. Wisdom should tell us to love, laugh, and make each day special, not only for ourselves but even more so for those around us. Wisdom should tell us this, but do we listen? Instead of listening to this wisdom, we become complacent with our time, our talents, and gifts. We ignore opportunities for sharing the gift of presence and, very often, the people and blessings in our lives as well. We take for granted that we always have tomorrow. We start this day out like any other hum drum day and hope to get through it, never intentionally making it worthwhile. Living worthwhile means something different to everyone; what does it mean to you? Think about it, make it happen; make it worthwhile, and Enjoy!

March 23

Good Morning Sunshine! Make it a Day of Remembering the Power of Your Words! We have been blessed with a voice and the opportunity to change the world and impact lives with what we say. We can profess our love or hatred, offer words of support or discouragement, voice our opinions, speak up for social justice, shout out in praise or in anger, and in the right crowd, silence a room with a whisper. I have heard the power of words, both good and not-so-good. I have witnessed the impact words have had on others, both words spoken in joy and in anger and pain, those that uplift and those that deflate. Our words have a far greater impact than we realize and affect more people than we know. We all know the sting of a sharp word, and the pain is not quickly forgotten. We also know there is joy in words spoken in love. Both can be everlasting. Remember the power you have with your words; use your power for good and change the world for the better! Enjoy!

March 24

Good Morning Sunshine! Make it a Find the Good in Everyone Day! Not always easy to do, is it? We, as a whole, tend to be a fault-finding and judgmental society. We can spot a flaw a mile away and often take pride in it. We recognize bad or wrong immediately. Yet, if someone spots our flaws, or worse, points them out to us, we become defensive; "They don't even know me, how can they say this or that..." Why is it so easy to find fault with others yet not have the ability to recognize our own flaws? Matthew 7:5 says: "First get rid of the log in your own eye; then you will see well enough to deal with the speck in your friend's eye.' No matter what others do, or don't, see in us, let us be a people who see and seek goodness in everyone first. Imagine how different our days would be if we took the time to seek out good qualities in one another? Some will be easier to notice, while others you may need to look a little closer or deeper, but it is there. Choose to find it, then point that out. Give a word of praise or encouragement when you see good. Everyone needs to hear it once in a while. Perhaps those who need a closer look haven't heard it in a long time. You could be the difference they need! See goodness in everyone, and Enjoy!

March 25

Good Morning Sunshine! Make it a 'Happy to Be Me' Day! Have you ever said to yourself, I will be happy when I weigh 10lbs less, when I get through this situation, when I complete this project? Maybe you have said, I would be happy if I looked like this person or that person, I would be happy if I worked there, if I had this or that, I would be happy if only.... Why is it that we are always putting off our happiness or making our joy dependent on outside sources? What if they never happen? Does this mean we will never be happy? Often, when what we have been waiting for comes along, our moment of happiness is exactly that, a fleeting moment, and then we look for so something else to make us happy because that is no longer good enough. What if we made the decision to be happy, joy-full right here and now, today? What if we realized that our joy comes from within ourselves and our relationships with God and others, and everything else is just icing on the cake? Today might just be amazing, hmmm, interesting concept! Psalm 118:4 says: "This is the day that the Lord has made; let us rejoice and be glad in it." Today is a good day to be happy! Be happy with YOU, today and every day, and Enjoy!

March 26

Good Morning Sunshine! Make this a Day of Being Still. Our Christian faith is both communal and private. Communal in the way that we worship together on Sunday mornings and when we join together in Bible studies, ministries and mission projects. Yet our faith also has a very private side. Jesus said in Matthew 6:6: "whenever you pray, go into your room, shut the door, and pray to your Father who is in secret." And, Psalm 46:10 says: "Be still and know that I am God." Only when waters are still, can we see deeply. Prayer and stillness are part of our Lenten journey. Listening to the voice of God is essential. Solitude is our effort to move away from distractions, work, never ending schedules, Netflix, email, social media, concerns about what others think, etc. We need time alone with God, in stillness, in quiet. I know this isn't easy for most of us. Living in our culture we feel the need to be busy all the time and usually when we stop, we sleep. Sometimes even when we try to "be still" our minds wander. Lent is this wonderful reminder that we need to take a step back, take a deep, cleansing breath, and open not only our ears, but our hearts, to hear what God is saying to us and to follow where God is leading us. Be still. Breathe deep. Listen, follow, embrace the journey and Enjoy!

March 27

Good Morning Sunshine! Make it a Day of Laughter! We take ourselves, others, and life far too seriously most of the time. We need to lighten up; we need to laugh and find humor and enjoy every day. I know many people are facing difficult situations, but laughter and humor are great ways to help you through. Did you ever laugh so hard that you are doubled over, your eyes are watering, and you have a hard time catching your breath? Don't you feel great after? Me too! Proverbs 17:22 says: "A joyful heart is a good medicine." So, if you want to feel better, laugh. If you want to get out of the dumps, laugh. You are already happy? Great, help someone else laugh today. Tell a joke, listen to others tell stories, turn off the news and watch a funny tv show, steer clear of "Debbie downers." You know who they are; if you are one, take a break from it just for today! See the humor in life. It is out there! Lighten up, be silly, have fun, find humor; laugh and Enjoy!

March 28

Good Morning Sunshine! Make it a Day of Playing. I once heard someone say, 'As long as you're playing, you're winning; once you begin keeping score, you lose. Everyone wants to win, to come out ahead, to grab the brass ring, to bring home the prize and be in 1st place, including me. It's a great feeling. However, there are some who will only play if they know they will win. There are some who won't even try otherwise. How do they know they won't win if they don't try? Half the battle is showing up and being part of the game. In this case, the game is life, and the lessons learned are from participating, being involved, and playing. Some days you feel like you win, others like you gave it your best shot, and you dust yourself off, and you'll try harder next time. Still, others that you feel defeated. No matter the result of yesterday, you gotta play again today. The reward is playing, not just getting a ribbon at the end of the race. Quit keeping score; just play and Enjoy!

March 29

Good Morning Sunshine! Make it a Sweet day! Psalm 34 tells us to "Taste and see that the Lord is good." This is not so much the taste with our lips but the taste in our hearts and the blessings in our lives. When you look at it this way, it may be more difficult to know the sweetness of God. Broken relationships can leave us bitter; disappointments can taste harsh and leave a permanent sting; our daily routines may be bland and leave us thinking life offers no flavor; is this all there is, where's Baskin Robbins when you need it? But the truth is God has given us life and the opportunity to season it how we choose; with bitterness or sweetness, you decide. Did you ever want chocolate so much that you tore your house apart until you found just one small piece? You didn't stop looking until you got it, and it was good! Well, sometimes you have to seek out goodness, but it's there! You get one chance to determine the flavor of today. Find the goodness, see the blessings even in the struggles, speak with kindness, never leaving others with a bitter taste, and truly know the sweetness of life! Mmmmm, Enjoy!

March 30

Good Morning Sunshine! Make it a Day of Giving It Your Best Shot! Giving it your best shot, best shot at what? Everything, of course. How often do we determine that today will be the best day unless we have some spectacular plans? How often do we try to be our very best at everything unless others are watching? There's so much we could do and give it our all, our best shot. We could decide to be the best parent, friend, student, or person. We could choose to be the best driver, shopper, employee. We could choose to see this day as the best day ever, no matter our plans, and have a great attitude and outlook on whatever comes our way. We could make our daily routines and same old schedules the best if we chose to. Usually, we don't. We just go through the motions. Obviously, we want others to see us at our best, but the truth is striving to do and be our best is more for us and is a result of the kind of people we are. Being our best and giving life our best shot is really defined by our character. Realize the significance of today and the brevity of the time we have, and the value in making it the best day for yourself and others around you. Strive for it, make it happen, give it your best shot and Enjoy!

March 31

Good Morning Sunshine! Make it a Day of Knowing That Love is Stronger! We know that no matter what life throws at us, if we are loved, cared for, and supported, if we know that we are not alone, we can get through anything that comes our way. I'm sure none of us need reminders that a lot comes our way, we are living in trying and uncertain times, but sometimes it is good to get a reminder that the love of God is stronger than difficult circumstances, struggling relationships, unemployment, loneliness, fears and anxieties, grief, or you can insert whatever has been thrown at you here. God offers each of us peace that passes all understanding, but God will not force peace upon us. God offers us unconditional love and amazing Grace, and it is ours for the taking, but God will not make us take it. God has shown love for us and offered assurance through Jesus Christ, but God will not make us believe. We need to do it ourselves. We need to accept peace, embrace love and believe with our hearts that we are not alone and that God's love is stronger than all of it. So it is up to you to do it, to know, accept and embrace the strength of God's love, God's everlasting hope, and God's peace that passes all understanding. Accept, embrace, believe, and know that God's Love is Stronger and Enjoy!

April

April 1

Good Morning Sunshine! Make it a Day of Knowing There is a Place You Can Go! One of my favorite songs is, "I Go to the Rock." Whenever I hear it, it's a reminder for me to turn to God in all things. We turn to friends and family to get advice, but if we go to more than one person, we usually end up with several different opinions, and we are often left more confused than ever. We share stories with complete strangers on the line at the grocery store because it somehow feels safer because we will never see those people again. We will solicit guidance through social media by googling our problems or reading self-help books. But how often do we go directly to God? There is nothing wrong with using all of those other things because I believe that through people, nature, and other sources, God's presence will be made known, but why do we go to them first? Matthew 6:33 says: "Seek ye first the Kingdom of God, and live righteously, and he will give you everything you need." We need to re-order our "go-to" list and begin with God. You may be led by people, places, and things, but it is important to know that you always have a place to go. Seek God first. Know, with God, you will always have a place to go. Go to the Rock and Enjoy!

April 2

Good Morning Sunshine! Make it a Taking it on by Storm Day! What if we were to begin our days thinking, not believing, that we are going to give it our all and take it on by storm. What is "it"? Life! "It" is this very moment today, tomorrow, next week, next month, next year. I can keep going, and I am so tempted, but I'm sure you understand what I'm saying! What if we felt as though nothing could stop us or get in our way? What if we had confidence that our contribution to this day and this life really mattered or had significance? Well, you do make a difference; you matter, and you are significant. Every day you make a difference in some way, shape, or form to someone, somehow, yet we doubt. From one child of God to another, snap out of it and stop doubting your abilities and start believing that God can work powerfully through you, and there is nothing you can't do! With God, all things are possible! Your choices are to give in, give up or give it your all! My suggestion, give it your all, take life on by storm and Enjoy!

April 3

Good Morning Sunshine! Make it a day of Marching to the Beat of Your Own Drum! We have heard the saying, "Dance like no one's watching, love even if no one's noticing, sing like no one's listening and live like it's heaven on earth." Gosh, don't we wish we could really be this kind of person? Who wouldn't love to not worry about what others think of us? How many times have you not spoken up with your own opinion because of fear of the reaction or response of others? How many times did we worry too much about the thoughts and ideas of others and went along for the ride because we wanted to be accepted and loved? God created us uniquely, knowing the very hairs on each of our heads. We weren't created to be exactly like everyone else. When we begin to live our lives embracing who we are and being more concerned about what God thinks and less concerned about what people think, the happier and more peaceful, we become. Hmmm, a God pleaser rather than a people pleaser, what a great idea! March to your own beat, BE YOU, and Enjoy!

April 4

Good Morning Sunshine! Make it a Giving It Away Day! Stop and think of all you have been blessed with. I realize some of you may need to look a little closer and dig a little deeper, but the blessings are there, I promise. Look at your relationships with partners, family, and friends, your health, a job, a house, a car, food, the air you breathe and the beauty of the world around you, your gifts, talents, and resources ~ I'm just getting started. Before you look at what you're lacking, count what you have and choose to share it to give it away! Don't be scared; I'm not asking you to give away your car or material possessions unless you want to, of course. But I am asking you to give away all that money can't buy because you realize what you have. When you count your true blessings, how can you choose to keep those blessings to yourself? Give away all that God has blessed you with. If someone is discouraged, offer encouragement; you can give that away. If someone is lonely, grieving, hurting, uncertain, offer your presence, a listening ear, and the hope of God's assurance. You can give that away. Give away the one thing that exceeds everything else~love. You can give away love in various ways through time, talent, resources, offering help, an embrace, or a word of encouragement. You can even say the words "I love you," to someone who needs to know they matter. Love and blessings only truly become ours when we share them. What good are they stored away. Give "It" away, share your blessings and God's love, and Enjoy!

April 5

Good Morning Sunshine! Make it a day of Being a Good Motivator! Notice I didn't say being motivated. Often the two go hand in hand, but they don't need to. We don't have to feel inspired to inspire. We can encourage, support, and inspire others around us no matter our own feelings. We usually feed off of each other. When you are positive, you have a better chance to influence others with positivity. The same happens when your spirit is negative. Now given the choice, wouldn't you rather help others to see the good in today, in life, in themselves and those around them, pointing out possibilities rather than what can't be accomplished? Ephesians 6:7 says: "Be enthusiastic as though working for the Lord and not for people." If we are working for God, this changes things a bit. Allow this to be your motivation to motivate others today and every day. Once you are motivated, think of how much more you can motivate others! Be positive, be motivational, be inspiring. Who knows, what you feed the world may actually come back to feed you! Enjoy!!

April 6

Good Morning Sunshine! Make it a Day of Seeing the Sun Through the Rain! We've been so lucky with the weather we've experienced through the mild winter and glimpses of spring, yet we're apt to forget those blessings and not appreciate our gifts. The weather often will dictate our mood, attitude, and outlook. When it rains, somehow, we allow it to put a damper on our spirits and our mindset. We'll often look back at the warmth of yesterday, or we'll long for sunshine to come, which isn't bad, but we forget to appreciate the gifts that rain holds for us right now. The same with many aspects of life. When life is going well, sometimes we don't appreciate it fully, or we can often forget our blessings. However, when the rain comes in the form of stress, fear, and worry (add your own rain here), we'll often look back at yesterday and say how blessed we were when the sun was shining, forgetting that if we look forward, the sun will shine again. It is written: "Celebrate the rain; it only means that the sun shall shine bigger and brighter than ever." Rainy days can make us appreciate the sunshine all the more. Challenging circumstances can help us appreciate the simple beauty and blessings in life. Don't let weather, gloomy, rainy days, or difficult circumstances stop you from seeing and feeling the sun! Look forward, see the sun through the rain and Enjoy!

April 7

Good Morning Sunshine! Make it a Day of Imitation! Did you ever hear that imitation is the best form of flattery? When we were kids, we hated it when someone copied us. How many times would we call someone a copycat or tell on someone for doing what we were doing? As we get older, the hope is we have a little better understanding of the compliment behind it. Now we, as children of God, want others to imitate us and follow our example as we live out our lives as disciples of Jesus Christ. Ephesians 5:1 says: "Imitate God in everything you do." Those around us watch us and do what we do. If we keep our eyes on God and do like God does, then others will do as God does too, or at least that is the hope. If others are going to follow your lead, lead them well. Lead them with love, with the hope of better things to come, with peace, with doing the right thing, with kindness and compassion, with grace and forgiveness. If you want others to love you, you do it first. If you want others to forgive, you do it first, and so on. Be a copycat; imitate God. You do it first and Enjoy!

April 8

Good Morning Sunshine! Make it a Day of Construction! Sounds like hard work, doesn't it? Well, sometimes life requires hard work, determination, and perseverance, and other times, it requires attention to detail and delicate care. What we are constructing doesn't so much involve manual labor, but it does require a commitment to complete what we have begun. So what are we building? Each other! 1 Thessalonians 5:11 tells us we are to encourage one another and strengthen and build each other up in hope. We are to ensure that not only we have a solid foundation of faith, but those around us do as well. We are to take the parts we have, like love, hope, joy, peace, compassion, generosity, etc., and put them together and build our faith and then add on by building community and relationships with those around us. Choose your words and your actions wisely to build others in their faith, and as you do, you continue to construct and strengthen your own foundation as well! Enjoy the construction zone! Happy building, Enjoy!

April 9

Good Morning Sunshine! Make it a "Being a Kid Again" day! Remember as kids we were innocent and pure in heart before we were jaded by the world? Remember when we could make anything fun and be silly and laugh? Remember it being okay that we were silly in the first place? Remember when our first thought was to love and trust those around us and not automatically assume there were ulterior motives involved? Remember when race, class, culture, and gender didn't matter because we saw and accepted everyone for who they were, well, except for the occasional boy/girl cooties thing. Well, every day that goes by, it gets a little harder to remember these things, doesn't it? Time, experience, people, and life has jaded us all to some extent and taught us to live more cynical lives. God reminds us that we must become like children, not naïve or immature, but pure in heart and mind. Be a kid again! Love everyone, laugh, be silly, steer clear of cooties and Enjoy!

April 10

Good Morning Sunshine! Make it a Day of Living in the Present! We tend to live in the past or in the future rather than in the present. Looking back at the past is great if we learn from it or if it reminds us of beautiful memories. However, we often get stuck there thinking of hurts and disappointments. When we look back wishing we were there, wondering how things would have been if only we did this or that, or the past hinders us from moving forward, we are stuck. On the flip side, looking ahead to the future is great if you have goals you'd like to achieve and you need to plan ahead in order to attain them. But sometimes, we are so focused on the final destination that we miss out on the journey and the people who traveled with us along the way. We need to let go of the past that we can't change and keep the big picture of the future in mind to keep us moving forward, but we need to embrace the present. Breathe in today, see your blessings today, take in the goodness around you today, and love the people in your life today! Live in the present! Today's going to be awesome! Enjoy!

April 11

Good Morning Sunshine! Make it a Day of Appreciating Nature! When is the last time you took a walk outside just to take in the beauty that surrounds you? When did you intentionally take a slow deep breath and appreciate the gift of air, the gift of life? God created the world for us, not just to pass through quickly on our commute but to take it in and enjoy it. We often take for granted all that we have been given, but we can be different today. Let's not just pass through or by anything. Open the windows if you can't get out or if you can go for a walk, touch the grass, feel the sun, listen to the wind or the sound of your footsteps on the ground, stare at the moon and the stars, get outside and take in all of creation. How can we not know that God is with us when we see, feel, hear and touch all that has been created for us. Breathe it in and Enjoy!

April 12

Good Morning Sunshine! Make it a Day of Not Trying to Make it All Make Sense! There are so many things that happen in this life that we just don't understand, and yet, we try to figure it all out. Why did this happen, why didn't that happen, how could things be this way? It is good to ask questions and wonder why and seek out answers and find reasons and some understanding. I encourage that. But the truth is, many things that happen won't have an answer that will satisfy our questions or will only prompt us to ask more. Sometimes there are no explanations, and things won't ever make sense. Our responsibility is to learn as much as possible, to keep asking questions and seeking answers. As children of God, we are to trust that God is in control and with us through it all to believe that we are not alone. Faith doesn't always make sense, but the peace in knowing the presence of God doesn't need to. When you have peace, you have everything. Having peace in a chaotic world doesn't make sense, but it is available. God provides peace that passes all understanding. Not everything makes sense; believe, trust, hope, find peace in God, and Enjoy!

April 13

Good Morning Sunshine! Make it a Day of Giving! We have so much to give that it won't cost us a thing! Ok, that's not true; it won't cost us money, but will take some effort, energy maybe even some time, but what you give will be priceless to others. What if you decided to give away as many smiles as you could today? We have an unlimited capacity to share a look of joy, kindness, compassion & perhaps even a look of assurance, but we so often keep it to ourselves. Did you ever think about your facial expressions or body language and the power they carry? We all know the difference between a look of disappointment and one of approval, the look of bad mood vs. a good one, someone who carries themselves with confidence or uncertainty, and no words are necessary to make this determination. 2 Corinthians 9:7 says: "Each of you should give what you have decided in your heart to give, not reluctantly or under compulsion, for God loves a cheerful giver." What are you giving away today? Are you displaying a positive or negative attitude? You are sharing it with others either way. What is it you want to give away? You are influencing the world just by being you, so be the best you possible. Give it away. Give the best of you. Smile and Enjoy!

April 14

Good Morning Sunshine! Make it a Day of Trusting! This isn't a problem for us with certain things, and we trust without even thinking about it. We trust morning will come when we go to sleep. We trust that we will arrive safely at our destination when driving. We trust that the water will be hot or cold when we want it to be or that our morning coffee will perk us up. We trust that our cable will be on during our favorite TV shows, and the chair we sit in will hold us. We trust in these things without a second thought, yet we struggle when it comes to trusting in more important things, like our own abilities, other people, and God. We doubt that we are good enough rather than remembering that we are children of an amazing God, that we are created with meaning, value, and purpose, and that we can do all things through Christ who strengthens us. We doubt, and we are cynical that anyone else can help us, that anyone will listen to us or will care for us, so we do things on our own rather than trusting others. And if people let us down, why wouldn't God? After all, I prayed, and what I prayed for didn't happen. Yet, Scripture says in Proverbs 3:5-6: "Trust in the Lord with all your heart and lean not on your own understanding. Acknowledge God in all your ways, and God will direct your path." Trust in the One who gives us strength and peace in times of trouble. Trust in God, who always keeps promises. Trust where it counts; start where it is most important, at the top. Trust God, believe, and Enjoy!

April 15

Good Morning Sunshine! Make it a Day of Not Giving in to Temptation! Trust me, I realize this is easier said than done, and many times, you sort of know that you're going to give in anyway. You see that shirt on sale, so you break down and buy it, or that new tool you have always wanted is on display in the window, so you look but then decide you can't resist. You want to eat just one cookie, but two would taste even better, or you can go over the speed limit by 5 mph or 7 or 10 mph. We have the choice to finish our work but right after our favorite show, or we know our schedule is already overloaded, but yes, I'll take on one more task and over-extend myself even more. We are all tempted by something, sometimes everything, and we often give in. Little indulgences are not always bad, but we can't allow small ones to lead to large ones. James 1:12 says that God blesses those who patiently endure testing and temptation. Temptations will come, no doubt about it. It's how we get through those temptations that matter, and getting through patiently is not the first thing to come to mind. However, seeking God's guidance, support from those we trust, and keeping our focus can help us stay on track. Don't give in; stand strong and Enjoy!

April 16

Good Morning Sunshine! Make it a Day of God Help Me! This should really be our every day, but we usually reserve our plea for God's help for those times of desperation, frustration, or even those moments when we speak the words through our gritted teeth in anger. The truth is we always need God's help, but we forget and try it, whatever "it" is, on our own. Our days should begin with praising God and asking for guidance, direction, presence, and strength to face whatever the day has in store. 1 Chronicles 16:11 sums it up, saying: "Seek the Lord and His strength; seek His presence continually." We are not to wait to seek out God when we feel like we can't do it on our own, but always. I don't know about you, but I can't do it on my own. Believe me, I have tried, but I haven't had the same peace in my heart as I do with God's help and presence. God is with us and is always seeking to offer us love, grace, mercy, peace, presence, and help. Don't go it alone. Let God help you! Enjoy!

April 17

Good Morning Sunshine! Make it a day of Being a Branch! I've been noticing the trees and the sudden changing of colors as well as the falling of leaves lately, as I'm sure you have. The branches of the trees are about to become bare, but they are firmly attached to the tree itself, the life source. Barring any unforeseen events, they will remain that way until spring, when they begin to grow leaves once again. However, an occasional branch falls, and it dies very shortly after. It reminds me of John 15, where Jesus tells us that He is the Vine, and we are the branches. If we remain in Him, we will bear much fruit, but apart from Jesus, we can do nothing. You see, we are just like the branches. At times we are full and growing strong. Other times we are vibrant and joy-full, and yet other times, it is as though we are bare and exposed to the elements and do all we can to hang on until we can bear fruit again. It is when we stay connected to the Vine that we will be sustained. It is not always easy when the elements of life are taking their toll on us! Stay connected to your life source, to Jesus Christ, to weather life's elements. Be a branch and Enjoy!

April 18

Good Morning Sunshine! Make it a Day of Not Being Afraid. In Mark 4:35-41, Jesus slept while His disciples were afraid because of a storm that seemed to be overtaking their boat. They even questioned Jesus, "Don't you care if we drown?" Well, as the story goes, Jesus tells the wind and waves to be quiet, to be still. And then he questions the fear and faith of the disciples. "Why are you afraid, don't you have faith?" Of course, they were in awe because the wind and waves listened to Jesus and calmed down. Ok, a long illustration, but fitting for our lives and our circumstances today. The wind and waves of the water can't compare to the ones we carry within us if we allow it. The problem is, we allow it. We can prepare for any storm, weather related or the storms life throws at us, but we are to have faith, not fear, that God is with us through it all. Jesus is helping to calm any storm we might face. Allow Jesus to calm whatever storms you may encounter today. Fear not; God is with you! Enjoy!

April 19

Good Morning Sunshine! Make it a Day of One Thing at a Time! This is not always easy. We wake in the morning with a 'to-do' list in our minds before our feet hit the floor. We are worried about getting it all accomplished, and we haven't even started. We don't take the time to give thanks to God for giving us another day to experience life, rather, we are just hoping to get through it. Our multi-tasking skills better not fail us now! I don't think it's abnormal, in our current culture, for us to think and live this way, yet I can't help believing that this is not what God has intended for us. God wants us to live and to live abundantly. The key word here is LIVE, not just get through! In John 10:10, Jesus says: "I came that they may have life and may have it abundantly." God wants us to live an abundant life, a full life! God wants us to experience the goodness of life abundantly and to live every day to its fullest. We are to experience God's presence through a sense of calmness and peace, through joy and laughter, and through the beauty around us in nature and in people. When our focus is off, and our minds are thinking of many things at once, we need to stop, take a deep breath, and focus on One thing; God is with us. You will need to be intentional about staying focused on God, but when you do, your thoughts, your attitude and outlook, and even your "to-do" list might change. Focus on one thing at a time, start with God, and you might just find that if you start with God, your focus might actually stay on God! Breathe, pray, focus on God and do your best to do one thing at a time! Enjoy!

April 20

Good Morning Sunshine! Make it a Day of Self-Medicating. Now, this is not what you think, don't jump to the wrong conclusions! We have all heard that laughter is the best medicine, and it's true. Proverbs 17:22 says: "A joyful heart is good medicine." Did you ever have a good belly laugh, and when you were done, you realized that you really needed that time of laughter, and it changed your entire outlook? There doesn't always seem to be a lot to laugh about these days. Tragedy and devastation, gun violence, Covid-19, protests, storms, the economy, politics, strained relationships, disease, the list of things to not laugh about is long and growing. Yet somehow, through it all, we are to live in joy and be cheerful. James 1:2-4 says: "When trouble comes your way consider it an opportunity for great joy. When faith is tested, our endurance has a chance to grow, and once we develop endurance, we will be complete." We have no idea what external forces will affect our lives today, this week, this month, etc. But we can control what's internal. We can control our choice to find joy in the face of adversity and peace in the midst of chaos! Be intentional and medicate yourself and others with hope, faith, laughter, and joy. Then heal and be healed! Enjoy!

April 21

Good Morning Sunshine! Make it a Day of Walking in the Shoes of Others. Well, we can't actually do that, can we? We can't have someone else's life or walk in their shoes. However, we can have sympathy, empathy, or compassion toward others. We can imagine what others are going through and wonder to ourselves what we would do if we were in their shoes or what needs might we have? We can humble ourselves and realize that at any given moment, our own circumstances can change, and we would look down to see that suddenly our shoes match the ones that others around us are wearing. We are not immune to life's difficult moments. Pain and suffering don't discriminate. We have different experiences, but no one escapes hardship. If you're wearing shoes that can walk to those in need, start walking, reach out and help lift others back on their feet. If you're wearing shoes that are tattered and worn, reach your hands up and allow others to lift you, shake the dust from your feet, start walking again and then reach out to lift someone else. Romans 12:15 says: "Be happy with those who are happy, and weep with those who weep." No matter what shoes you're wearing today, place yourself in the shoes of others and have a caring and compassionate heart. Give thanks that you have shoes and that you have life. Start walking, keep helping others back to their feet and Enjoy!

April 22

Good Morning Sunshine! Make it a Day of Embracing the Unexpected. Well, that leaves everything wide open, doesn't it? We plan our days and our lives, and we live most often with the expectation that things will go according to our own plans. Then storms hit, obstacles get in our way, people disappoint us, circumstances change, and our plans, as hard as we tried to stick to them, suddenly change because of the unexpected. Life can be confusing and frustrating, and constantly changing. During these times, let us cling to God. God is the one constant in our lives. If we do this, we can withstand, even embrace, the unexpected. In Malachi 3:6, God tells us: "I am the Lord. And I do not change." That's right, the whole world changes, we change, but God doesn't! Jesus Christ is the same yesterday, today, and forever. With this assurance, let us live as God intended us to live from the beginning, without fear, in joy, and praising God through it all! Be assured of God's presence, embrace life's unexpected moments and Enjoy!

April 23

Good Morning Sunshine! Make it a day of First things First. How many of us begin our days out of order? Well, we wouldn't know that unless we know what order we are doing things in the first place. The alarm goes off; we hit the ground running; so much to do, so little time. Before we know it, it's lunchtime, and we're getting anxious because the day is going by so quickly, and we're not accomplishing what we set out to when the alarm went off. Dinner time already? Yikes, now we're exhausted and in bed; where did the day go? We'll finish the things left undone tomorrow, gosh, that list is long. We'll say our prayers before we sleep; Dear G.....zzzzzz. Alarm, repeat. Sound familiar? This is why it's important to keep first things first. Prayer and time with God somehow make the bottom of our to-do list, but we always run out of time. When we keep God first, begin our day in prayer and reflection, and stay focused on what is true and right and Holy, everything changes. Our hearts and minds are connected to God and strengthened for whatever is next on our list. Do things in order, God first, then the to-do list. First things first! Enjoy!

April 24

Good Morning Sunshine! Make it a Day of Making the Little Things Count. We are so blessed every day, and we encounter the presence of God in so many ways, yet we often fail to realize it. We only seem to notice what we have after it's gone, then we complain about not having it rather than rejoicing daily and giving thanks. In the summer we are too hot. In the winter we are too cold. If it's Monday, we want it to be Friday....we are never quite happy enough. We always want big 'aha' moments that change our lives for the better. Me too, but when we spend our lives waiting for these rare moments and complaining between the 'aha' occurrences, we are missing out on all the little things that really bless our lives. The sun shining, the rain falling, the smile of a stranger, the embrace of a loved one, the sound of a child's laughter, holding hands, accomplishing a goal, helping others, receiving help, our homes, health, love, life, breath; all blessings filled with Gods presence. The little things are not really that little. Be sure to count everything as a blessing and make every moment count and Enjoy!

April 25

Good Morning Sunshine! Make it a Day of Sharing Your Smile! There is amazing power in such a small act, yet sharing your smile can make all the difference to the recipient. In a split second, a smile can offer peace, a sense of hope, or even the idea that there is love and joy in the world, all without a word spoken. A smile is one of the rare gifts you can actually give away that will cost you nothing but may be invaluable to someone who needed it. Smile as much as possible. Who knows, your smile may cause a chain reaction, and you just may get a smile in return that you needed to see. Do something radical today; change the world one smile at a time. Share your smile, and Enjoy!

April 26

Good Morning Sunshine! Make it a Day of Being a Trail Blazer! Frederick W. Faber said: "There are souls in this world which have the gift of finding joy everywhere and of leaving it behind them when they go." Have you ever given thought to what kind of trail you are leaving in life or to those who may be following in your footsteps? This is probably not our first thought as we begin our day, but perhaps it should be. Whether we realize it or not, when we encounter others, we are leaving an impression upon them, an impression they will be influenced or affected by and, at that point, one they can choose to emulate, follow or turn away from. Are you leaving a trail of hope and optimism, joy and laughter, or of love and grace? Are you leaving a trail that impacts the world in a positive way that others will want to follow and imitate? Or do others see the path you are on and turn the other way? Choose to be a trailblazer today, creating a path for others to follow and leaving behind joy, hope, peace and love, and Enjoy!

April 27

Good Morning Sunshine! Make it a Day of Taking Risks!! This is not to suggest jumping out of an airplane or trying daredevil stunts, but it will require risking our lives nonetheless. What if we take the risk of living life to its fullest, investing our hearts, minds & souls while using our time, energy & resources to better ourselves & others! Hmmm, we'd almost rather risk jumping out of the plane, wouldn't we? We often avoid risking anything because we believe we'll bypass hurt & disappointment, but without risk, how can we grow, learn, change, feel, love; how can we live? When we risk growing, learning, and changing, there's a strong possibility that we will become different people risking all we once knew for the unknown. When we risk feeling, we may experience joy, but we may also encounter pain. When we risk loving, we take the chance of either being head over heels or broken-hearted. Unless we take those chances, unless we take a risk, we'll never know what could have been. Only one way to find out! Take a risk; learn, grow, change, feel, love, live, and Enjoy!

April 28

Good Morning Sunshine! Make it a No Negative Thinking Day!! Am I too late? Have you had negative thoughts already? We get caught in the trap of looking for the bad rather than seeking out the good in most situations. We will notice the dark clouds rather than the silver lining and not think twice about it. We are suspect of people always believing they have ulterior motives, and whether we know it or not, others think this way about us. Why is it so hard for us to see goodness, to think positively, to live in joy, yet so easy to focus on the bad, be pessimistic, and live in a state of apathy or cynicism? Experience plays a big role in our attitude and outlook and has often been used as an excuse to support our negative way of thinking. To that, I say, stop it! Challenge what has been and choose to defy your circumstances. Be a people who live in hope! Our responsibility as children of God is to live our lives as an example of love, grace, mercy, and to offer hope, healing, and wholeness so others can follow. Trust me, that can't be done with negative thoughts! Pray, have a positive attitude. Think joy, live joy, share joy, positively, and Enjoy!

April 29

Good Morning Sunshine! Make it a 'Go For It' Day!! What 'it' is...well, you have to determine that for yourself. But I do know that if you don't take a step forward, you will always stay in the same exact place you are now. If you don't ask, you don't receive, and the answer will always be "no." If you don't go after what you want, you will never, ever, have it! We get stuck, and we don't try, and we don't move forward because we're afraid. We're afraid of rejection, failure, and disappointment, you name it, and it keeps us from experiencing new things. We do all we can to protect ourselves from harm's way, but there is more harm in not trying than in trying and having things not go as planned or the way we initially hoped. Is there something that you have needed to finish but keep putting it off? Is there a person you need to reach out to, but circumstances or pride have stopped you? Is there something you have always wanted to try but have been afraid? Joshua 1:9 says: "Be strong and courageous! Don't be afraid or discouraged; God is with you wherever you go!" If God is with us, what can we be afraid of??? Exactly!! So, take a leap of faith! The only thing stopping you is you; get out of your way, Go For It and Enjoy!

April 30

Good Morning Sunshine! Make it an I'm Beautiful Day! How often do we tell ourselves that we are beautiful? My guess is this is not something that just rolls off the tongue or a thought that comes to mind when thinking of ourselves. We are probably more familiar with having thoughts of ways to change our appearance, our body, our personality, and seeing or seeking out our flaws, but we never really see ourselves as beautiful. Why is it we listen to the media, take it to heart, and aspire to be something that's not real, and we get upset when we can't live up to the world's standards even though those standards are impossible to live up to. We hear our negative inner voice and believe it, but we find it so difficult to listen to and believe the positive and take that to heart. God created us and loves us for who we are; beloved children made to be loved and to give love. If God is love and created us in love, how can we be anything but beautiful? Tell yourself, 'I'm Beautiful' today and every day. Say it until it becomes a part of you, and you take it to heart; say it until you believe it, then live it! You are Beautiful! Enjoy!

May

May 1

Good Morning Sunshine! Make it a day of Feeling the Wind on Your Face! You know that first day of spring when you get in your car, roll the windows down and turn the music up and drive with your hand out the window and the feeling that comes with it. What a sense of freedom and the beginning of something new. There is an energy and excitement, a joy because it signifies a change for the better; more sunshine, longer days, warmer weather, and the ability to get outside. You know what I mean, it's freeing and peace-full. We should be living with this same sense of freedom and peace daily, but we often allow life events, disappointments, and letdowns to hinder that, and we feel trapped and anxious. Stop it! You have the ability! I encourage you to "roll your windows down" today whether you're inside, outside, or driving with loud music, or soaking in the silence. Be Free! Be Peace-Full! Feel the wind on your face and Enjoy!

May 2

Good Morning Sunshine! Make it a Dy to Leave Your Mark! I noticed a scar on my foot from a childhood injury. It left a permanent mark and a reminder of a painful moment in my life. Crazy enough, it made me reflect on the mark that each of us has the potential to make on the world. What impression, what difference, what mark do we want to leave behind that will make an impact in the lives of others? Will our marks conjure up painful memories or be a reminder that there is goodness, light, and love in the world? Our words and our actions are making a difference to someone. They are leaving permanent marks. Are they marks that inflict pain or marks that are leaving an everlasting impression of faith, hope, love, and grace? Either way, it's up to us to determine what type of mark you are making. You can and do, make a difference! You are touching lives and leaving impressions. Make them good, make them deep in love and overflowing in joy. Make them touch others in such a way that they are inspired to make their own marks that resemble yours. 2 Timothy 2:2 says: "You have heard me teach things that have been confirmed by many reliable witnesses. Now teach these truths to other trustworthy people who will be able to pass them on to others." Leave your mark and make those marks long-lasting! Go put your stamp on the world! Mark it up with goodness, and Enjoy!

May 3

Good Morning Sunshine! Make it a day of Finding a Good Bargain! We love a sale and getting a good deal, paying less, and getting more. We will invest our time and energy to get what we want for less. But there are times, in a quest to get more for less, that we get more than we bargained for. We don't read the fine print until it is too late. It is not just about retail; it is about life and relationships. We want more for less. What if we invested the same effort into finding a bargain into offering our time, talent, gifts, and treasures and reaching out to others. We are often not as willing to do this because there are no guarantees that we will get anything in return for our investment. Here's a secret, it is not about what you get; it is about what you give. Okay, maybe it is not a secret, but it is a reminder to follow the example of Christ. Jesus was and is the ultimate gift, the bargain, that through grace, provides us more for less; more love, more grace, more mercy, and forgiveness, all given to us free of charge. Follow that example, be the bargain others are looking for. Give away goodness, love, and joy; give away the gift of Jesus! Don't have conditions and don't have any fine print! Be the bargain and Enjoy!

May 4

Good Morning Sunshine! Make it a Day of Thanks Living! Thanks living? What does that mean? What if we live every moment of every day thankful for our many blessings? What if every day, week, and year became a genuine lifestyle of Thanksgiving! Why do we wait for one day to be intentional about giving thanks for all that we have and all that we are? My hope is this year, Thanksgiving Day will be the catalyst for giving thanks every day for the rest of forever for you and for me, and we change the day of Thanksgiving into a lifestyle of Thanks Living. There are many who struggle, that finding things to be thankful for, can be challenging, so let's start with what's before us; the air we breathe, the food we eat, our health, our jobs, water, the cars we drive, the clothes we wear......ahhh, there's so much to be thankful for! We may not have all of those things, but we each have some of those things. Even with that list, I believe the greatest gift we have to be thankful for is each other; the people in your life; for those whom you will spend this day with, for those that are far from you in the distance but close in heart and spirit, for those who have touched your life for just a brief moment in time and for those who have been a presence for a lifetime. Give thanks to those you love and have lost, yet, somehow, they still bless you for the privilege of sharing a portion of their journey of life and love with. Give thanks to those whom you are unaware the effect they have on your life, but without them, things wouldn't be the same, and give thanks to those you know make the biggest difference all the more! Give thanks to those who encourage and support you, to those who challenge you and help you grow, and for those who make you laugh or wipe away your tears. Give thanks that there are people with whom you get to share life and love with. Give thanks for what is most important in your life. And if you have not guessed it by now, the most important things in life are not things, but the people and relationships that you have. You see, it's the relationships, the encounters with others, that give life meaning and value. Stuff is great, and by all means, be thankful for that as well, but without relationships, stuff just doesn't have the same meaning! 1 Thessalonians 5:18 says: "Give thanks in all circumstances." Look around, take it all in. No matter your circumstances, there is so much to be thankful for. See your blessings, embrace them, value them, thank God for them all, and start Thanks Living today! Enjoy! p.s. I AM SO THANKFUL FOR YOU!!!

May 5

Good Morning Sunshine! Make it a Day of Speaking Kindness! Simple enough until someone annoys us. And boy, do people annoy us! From our family and friends to complete strangers, we get annoyed, and our words quickly go from love and kindness to words of frustration and anger. We often don't think before we speak, and we don't fully understand the consequences that can result from our sharp words. Once we speak, our words cannot be taken back. Ephesians 4:29 says: "Let everything you say be good and helpful, let your words be an encouragement to those who hear them; let them be a gift." If we thought of our words as gifts, would we use them any differently? It is inevitable that we are going to get annoyed and angry, and we can't control a lot of things that happen to us, but we can take charge of our words and use them to speak in goodness and grace. Let's allow our words to be gifts. Love and Kindness beget Love and Kindness. To speak kindness, you must think kindness. To think kindness, you must live kindness. It is a beautiful cycle! When we give a gift, we do it in hopes of bringing joy and sharing love. Let's use our words as gifts we are giving to others. Bring joy, share love, speak kindness, and Enjoy!

May 6

Good Morning Sunshine! Make it a Day of Hanging onto Your Peace! That's right; you have peace; it's in you and a part of you. You may not feel it, but believe it or not, you have the ability to have, to feel, to know, and to hold onto your peace! You may be questioning this when so much in life feels unsettled, out of control, and uncertain. So how can I be so sure that you have peace? Glad you asked! I know this because I know the Spirit of God lives and dwells within us, through us, and in spite of us. And if God is Love, if God is Hope, if God is Peace, then we must have all 3 living in us, through us, and in spite of us and our circumstances! Our problem is we allow strained relationships, life struggles, burdens, and situations to steal these gifts from us. You want them? They have been given to you freely; claim them, hang onto them, share them, but don't ever allow anything or anyone to take them from you! We are willing to give up hope, love, and peace when the odds seem against us, and we allow our peace to be stolen daily. Hope, love, and peace are already yours. Be intentional in believing in the God of hope and love and holding onto God's peace. If you believe in the peace of God, there won't be anything that can steal it from you! Believe it, hang onto your peace and Enjoy!

May 7

Good Morning Sunshine! Make it an Unconditional Day! We can be conditional people, can't we? We love it if people do what we want, love those we approve of, fit our mold, our schedules, and our lifestyles, and if they make us look good, that's a plus. We'll help those in need if it's convenient or if we like what we're helping with, not getting our hands too dirty or making too big of a commitment. We'll share belongings, money, and resources as long as we have leftovers for ourselves and enough put away for a rainy day. We'll forgive if others promise this or that, and we'll forgive, but we won't forget. It would be even more helpful if we actually like the people we're loving, helping, sharing with, and forgiving. Seeing our conditions should convict us of transforming our hearts. Aren't we blessed that we have a God who loves us unconditionally, for exactly who we are, the good, the not-so-good, with our flaws, shortcomings, imperfections, and all? How blessed are we to have a God who forgives and accepts us for who we are? We desire this from God and others, and we should love this same way, like God does, unconditionally. We are not loved because we're perfect; we're perfect because we're loved. Go love others as they are, unconditionally. Love like God, and Enjoy!

May 8

Good Morning Sunshine! Make it a Moving day! I read a quote by an evangelist that said, 'I am not moved by what I see. I am not moved by what I feel. I am only moved by what I believe.' When was the last time u were moved by what u believed? Our faith, our hope, and our belief in God should move us & transform us. Believing in God will not allow us to sit idly by and be stagnant. It will move us to do things and go places and touch the lives of others that we never thought possible. We will begin to be moved to speak up for what is right and for those who don't have a voice. We will be moved to reach out to help those in need. We will be moved to see beyond ourselves, our own lives, and our own circumstances. We will be moved to kneel in humility and prayer, thanking God, praising God, and seeking strength from God to guide and lead us so that we can be moved again. Pray, listen, and be willing to move, believing that God will take you places in body, mind, spirit, and heart to make a difference to and for others, to and for yourself, and to and for the Kingdom of God. James 2:26 says: "Faith without works, without action, is dead." Get Moving and Enjoy!

May 9

Good Morning Sunshine! Make it a Day of Leaving Yourself Wide Open! I know, usually, when we do this, it is the result of being the butt end of a joke. Today it has a different meaning. We have been jaded by life, people, and experiences, and we have become so cynical that we live closed lives. Let me let you in on a secret; you cannot live fully if you live closed. You must live wide open. Is there risk involved? Absolutely! Is there a possibility that you will be hurt and disappointed? Yup, sure is. However, there is also the great potential that good can happen. There are endless possibilities when you leave yourself wide open. When you leave your heart wide open, love is able to enter in and exit out easily, meaning you can give and receive love without thought and loving is something you will do without question. When you leave your mind wide open, you learn about the world and the people in it and gain incredible knowledge. Once you have the knowledge, you share it. When you leave your eyes and ears wide open, you begin to see and hear everything differently. You see people for who they are as creations of God, and when you listen, you hear that everyone has a story to tell. The Dali Lama said: "When you talk, you are only repeating what you know. When you listen, you learn something new." When you leave your arms wide open, you are ready to embrace people, and maybe, just maybe, they would want to embrace you back. When you leave your hands wide open, you are ready to give your gifts, resources, and talents to the world, and more often than not, you are willing to reach out with those same hands to help others. Leave yourself wide open. Live and love fully!

May 10

Good Morning Sunshine! Make it a Day of Letting Go of Your Past! We all know this is easier said than done, and why would we let go of everything that has made us who we are? Well, what I am suggesting doesn't mean not remembering your past, and it doesn't mean never looking back and reflecting on days gone by or cherishing memories or learning from things done, either right or wrong. My suggestion here is to let go of regrets, guilt, and those things that tether us to the past and prevent us from moving forward. We often get trapped by the past, and it prevents us from living in the present. We wish we could have, would have, should have, or that we didn't do or say something. Truth is, we can't change yesterday, but we have the opportunity to change today, tomorrow, and our future. Philippians 3:13 says: "I focus on the One thing; forgetting the past and looking forward to what lies ahead." If our focus is the past, that is where we will remain. If our focus is on God and what lies ahead, our potential is unlimited, and everything becomes possible! Stay focused with eyes and heart looking ahead, and Enjoy!

May 11

Good Morning Sunshine! Make it a Day of Begetting! Huh? Well, I am sure you have heard that kindness begets kindness, compassion begets compassion, love begets love, and so on. You want kindness, compassion, and love? Then give kindness, compassion, and love away. It begins with YOU! YOU start it! There is a catch, though; you can't give it away with the expectation of getting it back; you need to give it freely, without expecting anything in return. See, when you give it away, hoping to change others and getting something in return for your efforts, your motivation is all wrong, and trust me, you will encounter disappointment because not everyone will meet up to your expectations of returning these gifts to you. You need to Beget these gifts with the hope that others will be receptive and, in turn, do the same for someone else. Look for nothing in return. Then and only then will you experience those things that you are giving away, not because of what others did for you but because of what you did for you! Something inside of YOU changes when YOU show kindness, compassion, and love unconditionally. Better yet, do it because that is what God did, and continues to do, for us! Beget something good and Enjoy!!!

May 12

Good Morning Sunshine! Make it a Day of Being Beautiful! Don't fight me on this. I know many of you may be resisting the thought already!! Let go of reasons why you think you are not beautiful and hear me out. I don't want you to look in a mirror and find reasons why you don't look beautiful. Don't step on a scale to make sure your weight makes you beautiful. Don't ask others their opinion of you and think you are beautiful because someone else tells you so. Just Be Beautiful because of who YOU are and to whom YOU belong. YOU are fearfully and wonderfully made, a creation of God. How can you be anything but beautiful? We need to stop seeing beauty as the world sees beauty and begin to see beauty the way God does. God does not see beauty by outward appearance, through those rugged good looks, or that pretty smile, a great hair day, perfect make-up, or by the clothes we wear. Dig deeper, go below the surface and gain an understanding that it is your heart, your character, your thoughts, your spirit, and the love that you give away and receive that makes you beautiful. Be confident in your beauty. Walk with your head held high, knowing that God makes all things beautiful in their time and if you believe God created you, then believe you are beautiful. See you, and the world around you, as beautiful today. Be beautiful and Enjoy!

May 13

Good Morning Sunshine! Make it a Day of Searching for the Right Things in the Right Places! What is it that you are looking for? Are you searching for peace or to feel like you fit in? Are you seeking love or friendship? Are you searching for meaning and purpose or ways to fulfill your calling? Are you searching for answers to questions or for guidance and direction? We are all searching for something. Most of us are searching for peace and contentment. We are on a constant quest, whether we know it or not, always searching for more because we never feel quite satisfied. We are searching but are we looking in the right places? It's where we look that makes the biggest difference. If we look to wealth and material things, we may feel a sense of fulfillment, but it's short-lived, and we will soon need more and bigger and better. If we look to people to make us happy, it's only a matter of time before we are disappointed because they didn't meet some expectations that we placed on them. We need to search in the right places, to look within our own hearts, to search the scriptures, and to focus on our relationship with God. God's peace, love, forgiveness, hope, joy, grace… all of it is sustaining. You can't buy any of them, but they are all yours if you search in the right places. Contentment, peace, and hope can be yours, and it won't cost you a cent. In Jeremiah 29:13, God says: "You will seek me and find me when you search for me with all your heart." Search for God today, and you will find exactly what you need. Seek, and you will find! Search for God and Enjoy!

May 14

Good Morning Sunshine! Make it a Day of Having Faith in Humanity. We could also call it believing in others, or we can recall the second greatest commandment. After Jesus told us the greatest commandment, to love the Lord your God with all your heart and soul and strength. He told us to love our neighbor as we love ourselves. Somewhere along the line, we stopped having faith in each other, believing in each other, and loving one another. We have stopped looking for the love of God and the goodness around us. Perhaps we have forgotten to love ourselves, after all, that is how we are supposed to love our neighbors, isn't it? But, if we don't love ourselves, how can we love others? If we remind ourselves constantly that we are loved by God, and we were created in love (not just us, but everyone else too!), then we will begin to believe it. Once we believe it, we will live it. We need to be intentional in seeking out the love of God, in life, in us, and in others. I have seen it, and I know it exists, but I have made a choice to see it, believe it, and live it. I urge you to see it too! Seek it out, have faith and hope in God, believe there is love and goodness in others. Choose to see it and choose to have the faith and courage to live it out! Enjoy!

May 15

Good Morning Sunshine! Make it a Day of I'll Do It! Isn't it funny how we always assume that someone else will do 'it' whatever 'it' may be? I heard a song by Jack Johnson called "With My Own Two Hands." In it, he sings of changing the world, making it a better place, a kinder place, making peace on earth, caring for the earth, reaching out to help, making it a brighter, safer place. He sings of holding and comforting, but in the end, he says: "I can do these things, but you have to use your own two hands." What if we didn't assume someone else would do anything but felt within our hearts that we had to do something, that we would say, "I'll do it!" By us doing "it" doesn't mean that we work alone and add to our already busy lives, but perhaps it means we are to lead by example, teaching and encouraging others to use their own two hands. This is not to pass the buck, so to say, but to share the task, to lighten the load, and together loving, supporting, and accomplishing all that is before us. It has to start somewhere, don't assume it starts with someone else. Let it start with YOU! Say I'll do it, use your own two hands, and lead others to use their hands and say, "I'll do it," too, and Enjoy!

May 16

Good Morning Sunshine! Make it a Day of Having Fun! I saw the greatest quote yesterday that said: "live your life and forget your age."

Everything in life has taught us to grow up. In fact, when we were kids, it was one of our greatest desires. Remember saying the words? "I can't wait until I'm grown up." Then once we get there, one of our greatest desires is to be a kid again. We always want what we can't have, or can we? Our bodies may age and our minds (hopefully) mature, but our spirits can be as young as we allow them to be. I want to live my life and forget my age. I want to have fun and enjoy and embrace life as much as possible, don't you? Scripture tells us to become like little children, not to lack maturity, but to have a heart and spirit of simple faith and effortless abundant joy, a peace knowing that we are not alone, and the gift of innocence and acceptance. Children can have fun with anything and anyone at any time. They know how to live! We should do the same and follow their example. So have fun today. Laugh as much as possible, love everyone, be playful and silly and Enjoy!

May 17

Good Morning Sunshine! Make it a Day of Living Your Faith! Are you living out your faith? For those whose faith is in God, we are aware that God repeatedly tells us that we don't have to live in fear, but we do. God tells us we are not alone, yet we often feel isolated and lonely, even when people are around. God tells us not to worry because one minute of worry will not add time to our lives, yet we worry constantly. God tells us to lay down our burdens, but we continue to carry them, and instead of laying them down, we add more. God tells us that Jesus came to give us life, abundant life, yet we don't live like it. We often take our days and our relationships for granted, complaining or wallowing or assuming we will always have more time to enjoy life and the people sharing this journey with us. We all have faith in something. Is your faith in fear or feeling alone or in worry or burdens or taking life for granted? If so, reach out and talk to a trusted friend, teacher, pastor, or therapist. But if your faith is in God, then live like it. Stop being afraid and worried and lonely. Don't just talk about it; live your faith and hope that others might know the love of God through you and Enjoy!

May 18

Good Morning Sunshine! Make it a Day of Holding Your Tongue. When I was a kid, my brother would tell me to literally hold my tongue and say certain phrases that, if said under normal circumstances, would be fine, but while holding my tongue, the same words would come out a completely different way. He would tell my mom I said bad words, and I would get in trouble, and he would giggle. This is not the sort of holding your tongue that I am talking about. Do you know the greatest weapon we hold is our words, and we often use them to inflict pain. When we use our words to speak harshly, to belittle, put down or blame, I don't think we fully understand the pain we inflict. Kids who are bullied aren't usually hurt physically, but with words. We have the power to speak words of kindness, of encouragement, of love, of life, yet sometimes our emotions get the best of us, and we speak words of anger, judgment, and hatred. You have heard if you have nothing nice to say, say nothing at all. That's holding your tongue. You can build up or tear down, but once you speak, the words can't be taken back. Proverbs 18:21 says: "Words kill, words give life; they're either poison or fruit—you choose." Hold your tongue, use your words for good and to speak life, and Enjoy!

May 19

Good Morning Sunshine! Make it a Day of Carrying a Lighter Load. Why is it we think we need to carry everything on our own? Well, I have an answer; it's called pride. We want others to see us as strong and independent. No one wants to be seen as weak, dependent, or needing help. We don't want anyone to see us as less than. The truth is we were created to be in a relationship, first with God and then with each other. We need to understand that we are not meant to do things on our own and without help. When life gets difficult, and it often does, we need to follow the example of Christ and listen to His words. Pray! This is what Jesus did first. He went to a quiet place and spent time alone with God. In Matthew 11:28, Jesus says: "Come to me, all of you who are weary and carry heavy burdens, and I will give you rest." Yet we insist on doing it alone. Do you realize if you let go and let God carry you how different your life could be? You would let go of burdens, struggles and worry, and you might actually live in peace and joy, in spite of your circumstances. The presence of God often comes through others who will help us as well. Carry a lighter load, let go and let God, and Enjoy!

May 20

Good Morning Sunshine! Make it a Day of Prayer! 1 Thessalonians 5:17 says: "Pray without ceasing." That's great, but we can't have our eyes closed, and our head bowed for an entire day. This is impractical and unrealistic. How can one pray without ceasing then? Here is how it could work. Prayer should be so familiar to us that it is part of our lives, not something we set aside for meals or before bed or yelling oh my God when we are shocked, excited, or angry. When we face less than ideal situations, what if we just asked God for guidance and wisdom to lead us through it? What if we are faced with worry, fear, anger, or disappointment? We can turn our thoughts to God and react appropriately rather than on pure emotion. What if praying became as easy as breathing, and we just lived with an awareness that God is with us in every moment, every situation, every challenge, and involved in every aspect of our daily lives; our thoughts and words, and actions? If we lived believing this, it is possible to pray without ceasing. We need to believe the presence of God is with us in everything. Breathe in God, exhale everything else; pray without ceasing, and Enjoy!

May 21

Good Morning Sunshine! Make it a Day of Dwelling in Possibilities. "Dwell in Possibilities" is a quote by Emily Dickinson, and it is a quote that hangs on my wall. I read it daily and began pondering all of the things we dwell on, and possibilities weren't at the top of the list. We dwell in fear and worry. We dwell in self-doubt or self-pity. We dwell in impossibilities and things we believe we can't do or accomplish. We dwell in judgment, anger, and unforgiveness. We dwell in rote routines and mediocrity. We dwell in worldly things and not in Godly things. Scripture tells us that with God, all things are possible, yet we choose to dwell in so many other places and in negative thoughts, and they somehow begin to overshadow all of the possibilities and potential right in front of us. We need to challenge our thinking and move out of our current dwelling places and into dwelling in possibilities. When we were younger, we believed we could do anything, go anywhere, become whatever we wanted. The possibilities seemed endless. We need to believe they still are. Dwell in possibilities again, and Enjoy!

May 22

Good Morning Sunshine! Make it a Day of Light! Each of us has the amazing ability to shed light, to share brightness, and to illuminate the world. We are also quite capable of the opposite. We can make our surroundings appear darker and bring gloom to an otherwise sunny day. Have you ever known someone who lights up a room when they walk in, and their presence changes everything? People are drawn to light, to warmth, and to those things that can brighten their outlook and offer hope. The Scriptures are full of references about light. Matthew 5:14-16 says: "You are the light of the world, a city on a hilltop cannot be hidden, a lamp is placed on a stand where it gives light to everyone, let your good deeds shine for all to see." You see, we are supposed to shine the love of God for all to see, to provide light to those who are surrounded by darkness, to offer hope. If we, who claim that we love God, don't live out the Light we say we carry within us, who will? The world can be dark. Yet, we are charged with sharing the light of Christ, igniting a spark within others that they may shine too! Live brightly today. Shine and Enjoy!

May 23

Good Morning Sunshine! Make it a Day Filled with Lots of Laughter! Having a good sense of humor is a great way to uplift your spirits and the spirits of those around you, and it is healthy for your body, mind, and soul. Laughing has an amazing way of ridding you from fears and anxieties, it draws people to you and lightens our burdens along the way. Martin Luther King, Jr. said: "It's cheerful to God when you rejoice or laugh from the bottom of your heart." Did you ever have that type of laugh that was so good, a deep belly laugh? You laughed so hard 'til you cried, and when it was over, you felt lighter, happier, free. Psalm 32:11 says: "Be glad in the Lord and rejoice and shout for joy, all you upright in heart." Be upright in heart today, laugh as much as possible. Share your laughter with others. Perhaps you are not in the mood to laugh. Let me remind you of this, life and circumstances will always give us reasons not to laugh. Many times the alternative is to cry, but you have a choice. Choose laughter. Don't allow anything to deter or hinder you from living in joy. Life is too short not to enjoy the ride and the experience! Live today with lots of laughter. Laugh and Enjoy!

May 24

Good Morning Sunshine! Make it a Day of Appropriate Reactions! There are many things that happen and many people we encounter on a daily basis that elicit some sort of reaction from us. Here's the thing, much of our lives are not dictated by things that happen to us, but more soby the way we react in any given situation. Are your reactions appropriate? Are you quick to fly off the handle and yell in anger, taking your frustrations out on others? Or are you calm and think things through and react in a way that will foster peace or resolution? Either way, your reaction will cause a chain reaction; you fly off the handle, and you are likely to get the same in return. You speak calmly and possess a positive attitude and watch out because a positive attitude can cause positive thoughts and outcomes! Think before you react, and remind yourself to have a positive attitude, outlook & reaction! Galatians 5:22-23 share with us the fruits of the spirit: love, joy, peace, patience, kindness, goodness, faithfulness, gentleness, and self-control, keep these in your heart and mind and on your lips, and they will dictate your reactions! Enjoy!

May 25

Good Morning Sunshine! Make it a Day of Not Hitting the Snooze Alarm. If you are anything like me, you hit the snooze alarm several times before actually getting up in the morning (I hope you're not like me!). But how many times do we actually hit the proverbial snooze alarm in life? How many times do we put off doing something, thinking we will get back to it in a "bit," which turns into days, weeks, or even years. We tend to believe that we have all the time in the world, but as we age, we also look back and realize this is not the case. Today is happening. It's already started. Are you going to hit the snooze alarm of life today, or are you going to take every opportunity to live it to its fullest? James 4:14 says" "How do you know what your life will be like tomorrow? Your life is like the morning fog; it's here a little while, then it's gone." We are on limited time and need to live today as fully as we can. So, ok, that extra 5 minutes in the morning may still be necessary, but when it comes to living, setting, and achieving goals, just do it! Don't hit the snooze alarm on life. Live every moment and Enjoy!

May 26

Good Morning Sunshine! Make it a Day of Building Up! Wouldn't it be amazing if you could lift the spirits of others and make someone else feel good about who they are? We live in a culture where it has become the norm to judge others on every level. Guess what? As we are judging others, others are judging us! No one is immune! When we are not judging, we're just not noticing or speaking up. Yet what would happen if we paid attention and spoke words of kindness, not false words, people won't fall for that, but true words, in spirit and in love to build others up and encourage and support those around us? If you see someone and they're beautiful in any way to you, tell them. If someone does a good job, offer praise. If someone is having a good hair day, is wearing a nice shirt, if they have on a great perfume or cologne, tell them. If someone did well on a test or a project or sang beautifully, let them know. If you catch someone being kind or helping others, let them know you've noticed and share appreciation. Everyone needs affirmation every once in a while! Tearing down is easy. We need to build each other up! 1 Thessalonians 5:17 says: "So continue encouraging each other and building each other up, just like you are doing already." Encourage others today. You just never know who or what you may build up! Enjoy!!

May 27

Good Morning Sunshine! Make it a Day of Taking Action in Your Faith Journey! We fall into patterns of just allowing things to happen and have an attitude of "it is what it is," but I would like to give you a gentle reminder that it is what you make it! In order to make something anything of significance, it requires you to do your part, to take action, and to do something! The Book of James tells us that "faith without action is dead." If you have faith, then live it out! James also says if "you draw near to God, God will draw near you!" Matthew says: "ask, and you shall receive, seek and you shall find, knock, and the door will be opened." What these scripture verses have in common is action, work, and responsibility on our part. We want to feel the presence of God, but often we fall into feeling alone, isolated, and abandoned. Truth is the only thing limiting us from feeling God's presence in us. In Jeremiah, we are told that we will find God when we seek with our whole heart, again action on our part. A friend once told me God will move mountains, but you better bring a shovel! Where are you in your faith journey? Take action, do something, get a shovel and Enjoy!

May 28

Good Morning Sunshine! Make it a Day of Making Others Happier! I didn't say be a people pleaser; that wouldn't be good. But think of the people you encounter on any given day. Wouldn't it be great if you could make someone a little happier, a little better, a little more hopeful for having met you? Sure, it would! Mother Teresa said: "Spread love everywhere you go. Let no one ever come to you without leaving happier." The world is full of apathy and indifference, anger, judgment and hatred, and it is readily available to all. However, the world is also full of love and compassion, joy, acceptance, and peace. These, too, are readily available if you choose to find them. You will find whatever you are looking for, but you have a choice to be a dispenser and allow others to find something in you that could make a difference in their lives. It is all about choice! Do you choose to live in apathy and let others find love, joy, and hope without you or do you foster and facilitate those gifts that others are really seeking in life and make them better for having met you? Give away some joy today! Let no one leave you without leaving happier! Enjoy!

May 29

Good Morning Sunshine! Make it a Nothing's Gonna Stop Me Day! Would there be anything that you wouldn't try if you believed that there was nothing to stop you? Better yet, what would you try if you knew it could be accomplished? We often adopt the idea that when obstacles and hurdles get in our way that we automatically have to stop or give up. Have you ever seen a track and field hurdle race? The funny thing about hurdles is that you can actually get over them! Sure, sometimes you trip over the hurdles and fall, but I've rarely seen a race where the runner doesn't get up and cross the finish line in some way, shape, or form, even if it's with the help of others! They believed they could finish, and they let nothing stop them. They were determined to endure and persevere. James 1:12 shares that God blesses those who persevere under trial; they will receive the crown of life. Don't let anything stop you! Tell yourself nothing's going to stop you and live like it. If you fall, get back up and keep going. Obstacles may just be unexpected opportunities. Be determined to endure and persevere. Stop living afraid of all the things you think you can't do and focus on the obstacles in your way or the hurdles that look too tall. Just start running to get over them already! Don't let anything stop you! Enjoy!

May 30

Good Morning Sunshine! Make it a "What I Want to Be When I Grow Up" Day. Kind of crazy, right, since we are sort of grown-up already. But what if we haven't grown up to be what we wanted to become yet, is it too late? The poet, George Eliot, wrote: "It's never too late to become who you might have been," and Philippians 1:6 says: "God who began a good work in you will bring it to completion at the day of Jesus Christ." When you were younger, was there something that you wanted to be or do? Use these words of wisdom and truth for motivation to become whatever it is that we are meant to be. The trick is to never stop becoming or changing and transforming. God created us with all the potential in the world to live with meaning and purpose. We just need to believe that we are never too old to set goals and work hard to achieve them. I hope that even with our last breath, we will still be working toward becoming who we are meant to be! What do you want to be when you grow up? Perhaps it has nothing to do with vocation but the type of person you are; loving, caring, compassionate, generous, welcoming, honest, determined, joyful! It's never too late...become who you were created to be, and Enjoy!

May 31

Good Morning Sunshine! Make it a Day of Taking Time to Notice! We often wake in a rush and begin our daily routines without a second thought. Our focus is on getting out of the house on time or on our endless "to-do list." Until that's accomplished, we don't notice much, except maybe, how little time we have or how quickly our time flies by. Did we really focus on seeing how beautiful our lives are, despite our busy routines? Did you take a deep breath and give thanks for your life today? Did you think of why you love the people in your life as you said good morning or wish there were others around that you could say good morning to? Did you catch a glimpse of the sunrise, see the beautiful colors in the trees or the newly fallen snow and notice how beautiful creation is? Did you taste your breakfast if you had or made time for it? These are some of the most simple things in life, but did we take the time to realize their beauty and significance? Sadly, our focus is often blurred by the daily routines and requirements of life. Philippians 4:8 says: "From now on, brothers and sisters, if anything is excellent and if anything is admirable, focus your thoughts on these things: all that is true, all that is holy, all that is just, all that is pure, all that is lovely, and all that is worthy of praise." Do things differently today. Pay attention to details and understand the value of life and creation, of your many blessings. Pay attention to those you love and especially to God! Take notice and Enjoy!!

June

June 1

Good Morning Sunshine! Make it a Day of Being Yourself! You may think that this is ridiculous because who else could you possibly be today? Well, there are many who live in fear of who they are, fear that others won't like them, and fear of rejection. We then allow that to interfere with who we are and who God has created us to be. Dodinsky coined a term called 'You-Phobia;' "The ridiculous and absurd fear of being yourself when you let others' opinion of you matter more than what you think of yourself; this fear will hinder your growth and greatly diminish your chance of finding happiness." How true! How often do we care what others think of us so much more than we value ourselves and our opinions of us. Even more than that, we value what people think of us over what God knows to be true about us. Do you live with 'you-phobia?' There's a simple cure for that; just stop it. Begin to challenge your thoughts, be confident in who you are and to whom you belong! YOU are a child of God! You are fearfully & wonderfully made. YOU are beautiful and precious and loved. Tell yourself that! Believe it! Live it! Be yourself and Enjoy!

June 2

Good Morning Sunshine! Make it a Day of Having Compassion! When we, or if we, have compassion for others, it really is very telling about who we are. Compassion isn't just looking at others and feeling sorry or having sympathy but also having a strong sense or desire to do something, to change the situation, to help in some way, and to make a difference. If we want a true example of compassion, we can look to Jesus himself. Matthew 9:36 tells us when Jesus saw the crowds, He had compassion for them, and throughout the Gospels, Jesus had compassion for the poor, the outcast, the prisoners, the hungry, the sinners, the lost, the sick, the blind, and deaf, the children, those who mourn. Somewhere along the lines, we have all fit into at least one of these categories. Jesus had compassion, but He didn't just stop at feeling compassionate, He did something about it, and He urged His disciples to do something about it as well. You can't see a need and just walk by or ignore it. When you follow Christ, you are urged, because we are disciples, to DO something about it. Knowledge obligates us! Colossians 3:12 says: "Since God chose you to be the holy people he loves, you must clothe yourselves with tenderhearted mercy (compassion), kindness, humility, gentleness, and patience." We can't unsee those in need, although we might try! Have compassion. Feel compassion and Do something about it! Enjoy!

June 3

Good Morning Sunshine! Make it a Day of Unclenching Your Fists! A friend shared a poem by Madeleine L'Engle entitled "Epiphany" – "Unclench your fists, Hold out your hands. Take mine. Let us hold each other. Thus is His Glory Manifest." What is it that you are holding onto with clenched fists? What are you hanging onto that you are afraid to let go of? Your past hurts, disappointments, letdowns? Do you cling to your current struggles and situations and think they are impossible to let go of? We do know that if we let go, things will never be the same. Often, we are afraid to let go, so we hang on tighter and grip a little stronger. We find some sort of comfort and security in what's clenched in our fists far more than we have hope or trust that if we just let go, there is a possibility of an Epiphany, a realization that God is in control and we are not! If we let go, we just might encounter God and open our hands, our arms, our hearts, and our lives to the Holy Spirit and acknowledge that we can't do it on our own, none of it. Here is a little secret, we are not meant to do anything alone! God is with you. God loves you. God is in control. Let go already! Unclench your fists and Enjoy!

June 4

Good Morning Sunshine! Make it a Day of Working Out! Most of us will think of heading to the gym or getting on the treadmill. That's not a bad thing. In fact, I encourage it. A physical workout will increase your health, provide more energy and keep you in shape. But what if our workouts weren't just about the body, what if they included the mind and the spirit? Do you ever exercise your mind? Do you ever consciously give thought to your thinking? Do you question why you think a certain way or challenge yourself to change negative thoughts to positive ones? Do you read and do all you can to learn and grow in knowledge and stretch your mind every day? How about your spirit? Do you pray and spend time with God? Do you meditate on God's Word or gather with others to grow in your faith and spirituality? Having a complete workout is not just about transforming our body but transforming our body, mind, and spirit. We get to a point in our lives where everything becomes rote, and we become complacent in caring for ourselves. We have our routines down and can go through the motions without giving it a thought. Challenge yourself today to get a full workout; body, mind, and spirit, and Enjoy!!

June 5

Good Morning Sunshine! Make it a Day of Saying to Yourself the Encouraging Words You Would Say to Others! Why is it we always seem to have the right words to say to those around us who need support, encouragement, and hope, and we truly believe they have the capability and strength to accomplish anything. Yet when it comes to what we tell ourselves, our thoughts are of self-doubt, condemnation, poor self-esteem, poor body image, guilt, and shame, add your own words here. We are not very kind to us! You would never tell others the things you tell yourself! We need to change our inner dialogue and the conversations we have in our own minds. That little voice (or sometimes booming voice) can be our greatest asset or our biggest enemy. We get to decide. My recommendation is you should make nice with you! You are going to be with you for a long time, and life will be easier if you like you. Say the words to you that you would say to others! You are beautiful. You can accomplish anything. You can do all things through Christ, who strengthens You and believes in You. You are smart, strong, and able! You are loved. Encourage YOU! Speak to you with only positive words and thoughts. Say it until you believe it, and Enjoy!

June 6

Good Morning Sunshine! Make it a Day to Be First! In the world today, this is what we are encouraged to do and what we all strive for, to be first, best, ahead of the crowd, and number one. Well, let me just say that is not the kind of first I am suggesting. What if you were the first to allow someone to go ahead of you at the grocery store, first to smile, first to say hello and introduce yourself, first to offer encouragement or a compliment, first to offer your seat, first to help someone in need, first to reach out and make a phone call, first to offer forgiveness or love or grace, first to give your time, talent and money to a worthy cause? What if you were first and others began to follow your example? What if we were all wanting to be first to put the needs of others before our own? The beauty of this is without even knowing it, someone else would be putting you first at some point while you were thinking of helping out or giving to someone you put first. Matthew 20:16 says" "The first shall be last and the last shall be first." Be first; first to share the love of God by loving others first, and Enjoy!

June 7

Good Morning Sunshine! Make it a Day of Getting Aligned. We think of getting our car tires aligned, so they are parallel to each other and don't pull too much to the right or left but stay straight. However, hit a pothole or a curb, and the tires can be out of alignment. Tires, really? I know; hear me out! Did you ever think about checking your own alignment, your life's alignment with God? Are you caring for yourself spiritually and doing all you can to lead a life parallel to God's plan for you? Are you moving ahead in the right direction and not pulling too far one way or another? Today is Ash Wednesday, the beginning of the Lenten season, a time of taking a closer look at ourselves, our hearts, our minds, and our spirits and really examining whether or not we are in alignment and parallel in our relationship with God. It is a season to reflect, to pray, a time of confession, a time to ask for and receive forgiveness, to understand the sacrifice of Christ on our behalf. It is a time to align ourselves with God so that we can live, love, share, rejoice and move in the right direction. Check your alignment, and Enjoy!

June 8

Good Morning Sunshine! Make it a Day of Not Comparing! Do you realize how much time we spend (waste) comparing our lives to the lives of others? We are always looking at what we think others have, and we want it, but what we may not understand is what it took for them to get 'it.' Then we beat ourselves up because we don't think we're enough. We believe we're not beautiful enough, rich enough, intelligent enough, and we don't have the same gifts and talents or possessions as everyone else. We spend too much time comparing and wanting what we think we don't have rather than opening our eyes to the blessings right before us. We're each created with special gifts and talents, and we are not meant to be like anyone else in this world but us. Yes, we will have some similarities, but no two of us are exactly alike. Each of us has our own unique set of fingerprints to make our mark on the world that no one else can. If we're too busy watching others touch life and making their marks on the world, how will we ever leave our own marks, prints, and impressions for the world to see? YOU are God's creation. Stop comparing and start touching the world. Leave your mark and Enjoy!!

June 9

Good Morning Sunshine! Make it a Day of Better. We strive for that, don't we? We want a better life, better relationships, better experiences, to better ourselves...it is our desire, or at least it should be, to strive for better. Yet, somewhere along the line, we often find ourselves stuck in the mundane, living in mediocrity and just going through the same old routines. We become complacent and take things as they are, forgetting there is always the possibility of better. I read that there are 8 rules to a better life; never hate, don't worry, live simply, expect a little, give a lot, always smile, live with love, and best of all, be with God. There is nothing crazy on this list, nothing beyond our reach and think about it, if we accomplished any one of these things, we would already have a better day. One better day leads to better weeks, months, years, and ultimately, to a better life. If we approached each day, each person, each experience with this list it would change everything! Make it a better day and a better life. Follow the better life rules; choose better, and best of all, Be with God and Enjoy!

June 10

Good Morning Sunshine! Make it a Day of Fasting! I know no one likes fasting and feeling deprived, but what if there was a different kind of fasting that didn't involve giving up food or Facebook? Well, there is, but it may be more difficult than not eating chocolate. What if we fasted from saying I can't or deprived ourselves of negative thoughts, or we refused to ingest the judgment of others, or we refrained from worry, guilt, or doubt? If this were to happen, we just might believe we can. We might think positively about ourselves and others around us. We might love who we are while we are becoming the people, we have been created to be and not care about the judgment of others but live for God. We just might let go of control and live free from fears and anxieties without stress. We might actually live in peace. What if we fasted from our own thoughts and instead focused on Godly thoughts? Can you imagine, that this fasting thing may have its benefits after all!! Romans 12:2 says: "Let God transform you into a new person by changing the way you think." Fast from negativity, be transformed, and Enjoy!

June 11

Good Morning Sunshine! Make it a Day of Committing Random of Acts of Prayer! We've heard of random acts of kindness & I highly recommend that every day but have you just prayed for someone at random? We see people stressed out, upset, joyful & happy, or those who look lost. We know many who are going through difficult times, but there are others who put on a good front, and we have no idea what they're going through; your family & friends, strangers, those driving on the road next to us or sitting by us at work but do we ever think they may be in need of prayer? Whether celebrating or just trying to get through the day, there are dozens we could be lifting in prayer at any given moment, so why don't we do it, why don't we lift them in prayer? Human nature is to focus on us & what's happening in our lives. Change focus today; pray for those around you, at least one other person, at random today. They don't need to know; God will. You don't need to know their circumstances; God will! Look around; someone who needs prayer will be there. Commit random acts of prayer and Enjoy

June 12

Good Morning Sunshine! Make it a Day of YOU DO IT! We often complain about wishing things were different, or we take notice of where we are while wishing we were someplace else, but we have an expectation of others making 'things' different or guiding us to that someplace else or even worse, we have expectations of others making us happy. What if we actually put that responsibility upon ourselves and worked toward changing our own circumstances, or at least our own attitude toward them? What if we had a destination that would take us someplace else, whether that be a physical place or just a new place of understanding & peace from within, but we made our own travel plans? What if we determined that we create our own happiness and others can't, and shouldn't, be responsible for our personal joy? Others can enhance our lives, but they're not responsible for changing us and making us happy. WE are! YOU ARE!! Gandhi said, 'Be the change you wish to see in the world.' YOU want change? YOU do it! Others journey with us, but we get to choose our own path! Choose a good one! YOU do it and Enjoy

June 13

Good Morning Sunshine! Make it a Day of Going with the Flow! We start our days with schedules and agendas, to-do lists, and mental notes of things that need to be accomplished. But try as we might to stick to them, life happens, and plans change. We often become focused on what we have written down, on paper or in our minds, that we don't leave room for what today might have in store for us. When or if something comes up, good or bad, that was not in the plan, we get flustered, overwhelmed, and sometimes even angry. We want everything to go our way. Well, I am sure you are already aware this is not always the case, and things rarely go exactly as planned. These are the moments when we just need to take a deep breath, stay calm, think rationally, and go with the flow. It can be done! Isaiah 42:16, God says: "I will lead the blind down a new path, guiding them along an unfamiliar way. I will brighten the darkness before them and smooth the road ahead of them." How can we not go with the flow if we know God is with us, before us, beside us, ahead of us? If your day or your plans don't go as you had hoped, rest assured that God is with you. Go with the flow and Enjoy!

June 14

Good Morning Sunshine! Make it a Day of Discovering What's Special About Me! We're very good at looking at others and noticing what's special about them. We see their beauty inside and out and recognize their gifts and talents or their joy, kindness, compassion, or generosity, all of which make them special. But we don't often think about ourselves as being special. We are our own worst critics wishing we were like someone else. Well, we can learn from others, we can grow and develop, mature and transform but try as we might, we cannot be anyone other than ourselves! We have to live with us for a long time, so we might as well make the best of it and take a better look at ourselves and start seeing our own inner and outer beauty and our own gifts and talents and recognize that we are special. We have been beautifully and wonderfully created by God with meaning and purpose. Once we acknowledge that, we'll start living like we are special. Wouldn't it be a shame to live not knowing how special we are and not living up to our full potential! Examine YOU closely today and be determined to discover what's so special about you! Trust me, YOU are special! Enjoy!

June 15

Good Morning Sunshine! Make it a Beneath the Surface day! Isn't it crazy how much we value the surface, the outer layer, and only what the eye can see? We are impressed by clothing and jewelry, by cars and homes, and we think we know who someone is because of what they have. Equally, we are put off by these very same things if they don't seem to fit our standards. We are a fast-paced society, and we want to sum people up in an instant rather than getting to know who they really are. We hate when people do it to us, but when is the last time you said "how are you" to someone while you kept on walking? We all do it, we live on the surface, and sometimes we have to, but not always. Do you realize that life is all about relationships, and life is beneath the surface? We were not created solely for ourselves but created that we would live for others and in relationship with others. It takes more than seeing the outer layer to truly love and be loved, to help and be helped, to invest in others and have others invest in you. Dig deeper, Live beneath the surface and Enjoy!

June 16

Good Morning Sunshine! Make it a Day of Making it Happen! Our list of wants, dreams, desires, and hopefully, our goals is long. We want a lot of things out of life, but I'm sure you are aware that nothing gets handed to us. There's an old saying that says: "God will move mountains, but you better bring a shovel." We want something; we have to make it happen. We want our dreams to come true; we need to allow ourselves to dream and imagine possibilities, and then we have to work to fulfill them with God as our guide. We want to accomplish our goals; first, we have to pray, set goals, and then go after them. You see, it takes faith, work, effort, energy, time, a willing spirit, a bit of a fire inside, and a smidge of passion and drive for good measure. Then add in a ton of resiliency to get back up and keep moving forward to make things happen when we face disappointments or letdowns in our lives. It's not a question of us wondering if we will ever accomplish all we want and desire. The question is, what are we willing to do to make it happen? 2 Chronicles 15:7 says: "But as for you, be brave and don't lose heart, because your work will be rewarded!" What do you want to happen in your life? Today is your starting point to reach that goal. Tomorrow you may add to your list and begin a new starting point. The idea is to start, keep moving forward, living life, accomplishing your goals. Make it happen, and Enjoy!

June 17

Good Morning Sunshine! Make it a Day of Spending!! Woo hoo...who doesn't love spending? Here is a day we can all connect with! Wait, not so fast...I didn't mention money. I read this awesome quote from Ben Irwin, who said: "Most of us spend our lives as if we have another one in the bank." Yikes, this is so true! We spend much of our time and our lives like it will never end, or we spend it on things that are inconsequential or fleeting. Don't get me wrong, sometimes that's just fun, and we need to just have fun every now and then, but when is the last time that you didn't just give a bit of time but spent your time investing? When did you spend a portion of your day giving effort, energy, or your heart to anything long-lasting and worthwhile? Perhaps your list is long, and that's awesome. Yet, maybe you could have spent you and your time a little more wisely. We don't have another life in the bank, so we can't waste this one. We need to spend our time helping those in need, spend moments in prayer, spending time laughing, dancing, singing, being joyful, and enjoying the simple and small things in life. We need to spend our energy investing in us and our relationships with God and with others! Spend you wisely today. Invest yourself fully and Enjoy!

June 18

Good Morning Sunshine! Make it a Day of Serenity! We've heard the Serenity Prayer, 'God grant me the serenity to accept the things I cannot change; courage to change the things I can, and the wisdom to know the difference,' but have we actually read it, taken it to heart, and done our best to live it. This prayer is an expression of the desire to let go of the past, the courage to move forward with our minds focused on the wisdom, guidance, and peace of God. Isn't that what we all long for; peace, tranquility, calmness, and serenity? Don't we want to know when to let go and let God? Life's circumstances aren't always going to bring about any of these; however, if we know when to let go, what we're doing is choosing to live in peace no matter what's happening around us. We forget that we can choose peace when the world seems to be pressing in on us. We can choose tranquility during trials. We can choose calmness in the midst of chaos. We can choose to humbly ask God for serenity, courage and wisdom, and then believe they belong to us, take hold of them & live with serenity. Embrace God's peace and Enjoy!!

June 19

Good Morning Sunshine! Make it a day of Looking Inside! I read a quote from Eckhart Tolle that said: "Stop looking outside for scraps of pleasure or fulfillment, for validation, security or love – you have a treasure within that is infinitely greater than anything in the world." We are always looking to outside sources for our own self-worth and value. If others believe us to be beautiful, intelligent, and worthy and tell us often enough, we will accept it, at least for a while. While these things are true of each of us, that we are beautiful, intelligent, and worthy, we are seeking scraps, as Tolle put it because we are looking in the wrong places for validation, and we will want or need, others to tell us again and again, so we stay happy. It's great to be given a compliment; it makes us feel good, and we should be quick to lift each other up. However, if we only listen to what others tell us as our source of affirmation, we are in trouble because we are not always going to hear what we want, or need, to hear. Might I suggest that we look to God for validation; you will find much more than scraps. God calls us child, friend, and tells us that we have been justified and redeemed, that we are new creations who have been forgiven and freed, and we are God's treasure. Look to God, listen to God, then look inside your heart; you will find your treasure...YOU! Enjoy!

June 20

Good Morning Sunshine! Make it a Day of Until! Until, by definition, means "up to a time that or when." After giving this word, Until, some contemplation, it seems as though we could use this word at the end of many of our thoughts; I will try until, work until, give until, forgive until, help until, reach out until, live until, love until... You see what I mean? If we lived Until the point that or when, whatever it is that we want or desire, it means that we are not giving up but will keep going 'Until' it happens. We'll try until we succeed, work until goals are achieved, forgive until hearts are at peace, help until others are blessed by our words, resources, and actions, reach out until the needs of others are met, live fully embracing life until....Love as much as possible until.....How long should you try? Until. How long should you work? Until. How much should you give? Until. How often should you forgive? Until. How much do you help or reach out? How fully should you live and love? Until!! Do it all up to the point that or when...do it Until and Enjoy!

June 21

Good Morning Sunshine! Make it a Day of Because You Can! Smile today because you can! Be kind and share kind words with others because you can! Help someone, anyone, today because you can! Believe in you, your gifts and talents, and your abilities because you can! Live in peace because you can! Choose to have positive thoughts and a positive attitude because you can! Believe you have been created with meaning and purpose because you can. Love; love God, love others, love yourself, because you can! Choose to do all of these and to live your life fully today and every day because you can! Some will argue and change the word "can" to "can't," but why would we do that? We believe what we tell ourselves, so why wouldn't we tell ourselves we can? We have that option! If we believe we can, we have already won half the battle! We often fall into the trap of "I can't" and believe we can't far too often. Challenge your thoughts and remove "I can't" from your vocabulary! Philippians 4:13 says: "I CAN do all things through Christ who strengthens me." Believe you can, live like you can, because you can, and Enjoy!

June 22

Good Morning Sunshine! Make it a Day of Knowing What You Want! We have all been created with meaning and purpose. Some of us may already know what that is, some are in the discovery process, and some of us still don't have a clue. In any event, knowing our purpose, working toward it, or being uncertain, if we don't know what we actually want out of life, how can we ever work toward it and fulfill our purpose. When we don't know what we want, we flounder and live with uncertainty without goals and direction. Did you ever ask yourself what you want out of life? That may be a lot to ponder, but something we need to think about. What is it that you want out of the next year or the next month? Let's start on a smaller scale. What is it that you want out of today? What would you like to realistically accomplish or achieve before the days end? Make your mind up and work toward it. Be determined. Maybe you just want to be happy, then do it. If you don't feel happy, guess what, you have the power to challenge your own emotions and choose to be happy. Perhaps you want to help others; start, one person, one cause, at a time. Do you want to go to school, get a new job, meet new people, or travel? Whatever it is, know what you want, work toward it and Enjoy!

June 23

Good Morning Sunshine! Make it a Day of Knowing YOU are loved! We all like to hear the words 'I love you', and even more than hearing the words, we like to know through actions that we are loved. It's not only what is said; actions and words need to be in alignment. Well, the truth is we may not always be told, and we may not always be shown in ways we are hoping for, but we need to remind ourselves how much we are loved to the point we know it, whether it is spoken or demonstrated to us by others, or not. We need to remind ourselves that God loves us! Zephaniah 3:17 say: "God is living among you. He is a mighty savior. He will take delight in you with gladness, with his love he will calm all your fears. He will rejoice over you with joyful songs," and Psalm 136:26 says: "Give thanks to God of heaven for his steadfast love endures forever." Life and people may not always make us feel loved. When that is the case, we need to dig deeper, to seek God, and to know this amazing love. Once we know the love of God, we may even want to give it away. Often what we give away has a way of coming back to us! YOU are loved! Know it, believe it, live it, give it away and Enjoy!

June 24

Good Morning Sunshine! Make it Day of No Wrinkles! I think worry and stress cause wrinkles, don't you? Many of us are worriers by nature; we worry if we will look good enough, if we will make it to here or there on time, did we do this or that right. We worry about friends and family and the family and friends of our friends and family. We worry about the economy and what is going on in the world. We worry about things that are inconsequential and out of our control. We worry about everything!!! We spend so much of our time worrying that it becomes detrimental to our living. Worry is so bad for our health and wellbeing and is harmful to us spiritually, emotionally, mentally, and physically. What I'm suggesting is that when you find yourself in a place of worry that you ask yourself, "will this matter in 5 years?" If it will matter, stop worrying and be proactive and do what you can to change, face, or better the situation. If it won't matter in 5 years, move on and let it go! Matthew 6:27 says, "Can any one of you by worrying add a single hour to your life?' We can't add hours to our lives by worrying, but I bet we can add wrinkles. Don't do it! Be worry and wrinkle-free and Enjoy!

June 25

Good Morning Sunshine! Make it a Day of Believing You Make a Difference! We may never fully realize the impact we have on the world, the lives we touch or affect by our words and our actions. God will often use us to share love, mercy, compassion, and grace, and we may not even know it. Actually, that's ok; we don't need to know it. We just need to be willing vessels to allow it to happen. We very often underestimate the gifts we possess or the potential we have to impact the world, one person at a time. There is incredible power in a gentle touch or embrace. Sharing a smile can change someone's day. Offering a kind word or a sincere compliment can lift spirits. Listening and being a presence for another can be that reminder that they're not alone and provide peace and comfort. It is the smallest, simplest acts of caring that make the biggest difference in our lives. To know we're loved and cared for, and we're not alone is what we all strive for. You can be that difference for someone else; believe it and live as though you matter, and make a difference~YOU DO! Enjoy!

June 26

Good Morning Sunshine! Make it a Day of Recognizing Your Self-Worth! I read that some people will like you for no reason, and some people will not like you for no reason. What we believe about ourselves lies somewhere in between. Who we choose to spend most of our time with, those we spend our thoughts and effort on often, will determine exactly how much we like ourselves. We should surround ourselves with positive energy, which includes our own thoughts and attitudes as well as those of others around us. We draw from each other. Positive energy will create positive energy but so will negative energy. If only we could see ourselves as God sees us, it would change our view of our own self-worth. It would change the way we love ourselves and others. Honestly, it would change everything because our confidence and our daily approach to life would be so different. If we truly believe in the power of God's love for us, we would never question how much we are loved and valued, and we would know our worth. We choose to see ourselves through the eyes of the world, but wouldn't it be great to see ourselves through the lens of God's eyes for just a moment? God sees us as beloved children, wonderfully made, salt of the earth, and the light of the world, chosen and loved. Why is it we can't see what God sees? God loves you! You are worthy. You are loved! Know your self-worth. Believe it and live it! Enjoy!

June 27

Good Morning Sunshine! Make it a 'Bigger Day!' Well, most of us don't want to think in terms of bigger, do we? I usually don't either, but today I'm suggesting that we should all live Bigger! Make it a day when your faith is bigger than your fear, your confidence is bigger than your self-doubt, and your willingness to forgive is bigger than the pain of holding a grudge. Make it a day where your love is bigger than hatred, anger, or apathy, your trust in God is bigger than your problems, and your hope for the future is bigger than your circumstances. We have become so used to big issues and small living, and that's just not how life is supposed to be. We should be living Bigger! We have a Big God who loves us in Big ways, yet we don't live that way! John 10:10 Jesus says: "I came that they may have life and have it abundantly." Abundantly??? And we have been living small all this time? We live in a Big beautiful world and have been given some Big blessings, and we need to choose to let go of the small living and begin living large, abundantly; we need to live Bigger and Enjoy!

June 28

Good Morning Sunshine! Make it a Day of Adoption! Yup, you read that right, adoption! If you've ever looked up the meaning of the word 'adopt,' it says to choose or take as one's own; make one's own by the selection, to take or receive into any kind of new relationship. So, yes, this should be adoption day! A day to choose, to adopt! Let's adopt a positive attitude, choosing to make it our own! Let's adopt a spirit of love & generosity, making them both part of who we are; loving & generous people. Let's adopt the outlook that we're going to live happy and productive lives no matter who tells us we can't or if obstacles get in our way; let's adopt determination & perseverance! Let's adopt the belief that God is with us through it all, and we have no reason to fear because we're not alone; we can do all things through Christ who strengthens us! Many have adopted an attitude of being discouraged & defeated, but here's the thing with adoption-YOU get to choose what you're adopting! Choose to adopt wisely; a spirit & attitude to propel you forward and Enjoy!

June 29

Good Morning Sunshine! Make it a Prison Break Day! How many of us are prisoners and held captive? While it is true we may not be locked behind bars with a tin cup singing "nobody knows the trouble I've seen" (please excuse my memories from old movies), there are many who hold themselves hostage. There are those who feel trapped with guilt and condemnation, with self-doubt and low self-esteem, those who lack confidence, or simply many who feel isolated. Still, others feel trapped by circumstances. We hold ourselves captive far too often, and the only way to escape is to break out! Galatians 5:1 says: "Christ has set us free to live a free life. So take your stand! Do not let yourselves be burdened again by the yoke of slavery." If Jesus came to set us free, why do we incarcerate ourselves with negative thoughts and emotions? The freedom that God offers us through Christ comes from within but to find it, you've got to break free from negativity to experience that freedom, and then you need to hang onto it! Break free from negative emotions, thoughts, and actions today and find refuge in God, and Enjoy!

June 30

Good Morning Sunshine! Make it a Day of Sharing the Light! Have you ever been in a dark room with just the flame of a match or a candle? No matter how dark it is, you can still see a glimmer of light. If your life was like this flame, would others see the light in the darkness because of you? How many others would catch fire in your presence because you didn't keep the flame to yourself but rather, you shared your fire? Would your happiness and joy radiate and illuminate your surroundings and draw others in to share in the warmth? Do you ignite the flames of others and help keep their flames burning brightly? John 1:5 says: "The light shines in the darkness, and the darkness can never extinguish it." You possess the most beautiful light, the light of Jesus Christ! If you don't share this brilliant light with the world, who will? Whether you are blazing brightly or you are simply a match trying to stay lit in the rush of air that we often get caught up in with life circumstances, our light needs to stay bright that others may follow. Share the light, ignite flames and Enjoy!

July

July 1

Good Morning Sunshine! Make it a Day of Never! We have heard the quote "never say never," but today, I am going to encourage you to say "never" to many things. Never believe you are too old or too young to set and accomplish goals! Never take life too seriously. Never worry about failing; have the courage to try everything! Never stop dreaming. Never doubt that you are loved and that you were created out of love to live a full and abundant life with meaning and purpose! Never lack faith; question it, seek deeper meaning but never let go. Never lose heart but live with the certainty of hope that you are more than your circumstances. Circumstances are temporary; hope is eternal. Never let the odds against you keep you from moving forward or rising above! Galatians 6:9 says: "Never tire of doing good. At just the right time, we will reap a harvest of blessing if we don't give up." So, never, never, never give up! Never stop believing in the promises of God. We never have to live in fear, and we are never alone! Never lose sight of blessings and never take life for granted! Never stop embracing love, and Enjoy!

July 2

Good Morning Sunshine! Make it a Loving Your Life Day! I read a quote that resonated with me: "Your Mission: Be so busy loving your life you have no time for hate, regret, or fear." We spend, or should I say, waste, so much of our time hating, regretting, and living in fear. We hate people and the way they dress and live and for their own personal choices that we have no control over. We hate our jobs and circumstances and often ourselves. We regret our past decisions, things we have done or said, or things we have left unfinished or unspoken, and we carry those burdens. Heavy, aren't they? We live in fear of making more bad decisions, so we make no decisions and become stagnant. We fear losing good relationships and letting go of bad ones. We fear rejection on every level; we get to the point that we actually begin to fear living, truly living. Why? Because we have to risk, and we think, "what if it's too good to be true?" We are afraid, so we hate and regret and live fearfully. Stop it! You have one life to live, beginning today. You can't dwell in the past, and you can't change it, but you can learn from it! Get so busy loving your life that there is no room for anything but love. Go on, give it a try. Erin Hanson wrote: "There is freedom waiting for you, on the breezes of the sky. And you ask, "What if I fall?" Oh, but my darling, "What if you fly?" Love your life, learn to fly, and Enjoy!

July 3

Good Morning Sunshine! Make it an Extraordinary Day! We go through our lives living the ordinary, not fully comprehending how special, beautiful, and extraordinary our lives are. Do you ever take notice, I mean really look closely, at the people in your life; family, friends, and loved ones and think how blessed you are to be surrounded by those who love you and that you are able to love in return? That's extraordinary! Did you ever think about the work you do? We sometimes believe it to be mundane and boring, and many actually dislike what they do. However, if you work with a smile on your face, the love of God in your heart, and believe what you do makes a difference, then that is extraordinary! There is no ordinary work!! Take more than a glimpse at your life today, and all that's around you and find the extraordinary in it! The fact that you are alive and breathing makes today extraordinary! Don't miss out on all the blessings that God has in store for you by seeing your life and approaching this day, or any day, as ordinary! Embrace life as an amazing gift and live extraordinarily! Enjoy!

July 4

Good Morning Sunshine! Make it a Day of Making the World Come Alive! Howard Thurman wrote, "Don't ask yourself what the world needs, ask yourself what makes you come alive, and then go do it. Because the world needs people who have come alive!" How brilliant a thought... and even more brilliant if we live it!! What is it that would make you come alive? What would ignite your spirit and uplift your soul? Just think about it, if we were to come alive and really love life and everyone and everything around us, how can we not invigorate life into others? It would be impossible not to! Don't you feel more energized when you encounter others who radiate positive energy and enthusiasm with those who are truly alive? Sure, you do; we all do! It's contagious! Do you realize you have the same ability as those people? The only thing stopping you is you and your attitude and outlook on life! Come alive today! Breathe deeper, smile bigger, laugh louder, hug stronger, dance somewhere, anywhere, love fuller, and sing with joy! Come alive, so others can catch what you've got, and Enjoy

July 5

Good Morning Sunshine! Make it a Day of Believing it is a Wonderful Life! Remember the movie? George Bailey has a wonderful life but somehow allows circumstances to cloud his vision of all he has, and he can only see what he's missing, and it puts him in a place of darkness and despair to the point he wishes he had never been born. You know the story. In the end, he realizes the true riches in life and all the blessings that were always right in front of him and readily available, and he was never alone. It was a wonderful life. I bet he had only wished he realized it sooner. I know it is just a movie but how many of us wake in the morning and see our blessings and really believe our day and life will be wonderful? Do you see all the riches you possess and know that you are not alone? Wouldn't it be better to know how wonderful life is today, here and now, rather than look back and see how wonderful it was and wish you had realized it sooner? Of course! You have a wonderful life. Choose to realize it today. If you don't think life is wonderful, make changes. You have the power to do that. Make life wonderful, and Enjoy!

July 6

Good Morning Sunshine! Make it a Day of Work! Work? Seriously? Of all the things today could be about, the last thing we would want it to be about is work. Thomas Edison said opportunity is missed by most people because it's dressed in overalls and looks like work. We live in a society that wants instant gratification and the most benefit for the least amount of effort. Sounds great; sign me up! We know this is unrealistic and anything worth having is worth working for. Opportunities will present themselves to us time and time again. Many will allow the moment of opportunity to pass rather than seizing it and taking advantage of a chance because instead of seeing possibilities, they will see hard work, effort, obstacles, and excuses that will all overshadow vision, and many will give up. After all, no one wears overalls and rolls up their sleeves anymore, right? No one likes to sweat and work hard, so we just wait for another, easier opportunity to appear; sometimes they do, sometimes they don't. The greatest opportunity, though, is living your life. You have to fight for it, work hard for it and wear overalls and work for what you want. Colossians 3:23-24 says: "Do your work willingly, as though you were serving the Lord himself, and not just your earthly master. In fact, the Lord Christ is the one you are really serving, and you know that he will reward you." When you commit your work, whatever your work is, to Jesus, you will be rewarded. So, work to reach your goals. It's worth it! You are worth it! Work hard and Enjoy!!

July 7

Good Morning Sunshine! Make it a Day of Hanging onto Truth! Did you ever notice that we hang onto what was or what used to be? We hang onto the past like we can change it. We tend to hang onto people and relationships that aren't always good for us. We hang on to seeking acceptance, approval, or validation from those who will never provide what we are longing for. We hang onto negative feelings of insecurity, unworthiness, and anger. Why is it we hang onto all these things that we have convinced ourselves to be true when God has clearly stated and demonstrated truth to us? God has told us that we are loved and that we are created from love; we should be hanging onto that. God sent Jesus to demonstrate love for us. This is what we should hang onto! These are the things we should know to be true. We are fearfully and wonderfully made, created in the image of God, in the image of love, and we are never alone! When we let go of these truths, we find ourselves listening to things that aren't true about us, about others, and about the world around us. Zephaniah 3:17 says: "The Lord your God is with you, he is mighty to save. He will take great delight in you; he will quiet you with his love, he will rejoice over you with singing." This is the truth! When you are not sure what to believe anymore, read that scripture again. Believe it! Hang onto it and Enjoy!

July 8

Good Morning Sunshine! Make it a Day of Seeing Beyond Imperfections! We're so quick to notice flaws. We can find shortcomings, inadequacies, and faults in everyone and everything, including ourselves, especially ourselves. Then we wonder why we live unhappy or disappointed. If all we're seeing is what's missing, lacking, wrong, or imperfect, then, of course, we'll never be happy. Being happy doesn't mean that everything is perfect; it's a choice to look beyond imperfections and shortcomings. Being happy is the result of embracing and appreciating what we have and seeing beyond what we think we're missing. Mignon McLaughlin wrote: "We're seldom happy with what we have now but would go to pieces if we lost any part of it." We find our lives less than perfect, maybe they are, but perhaps they're more perfect than we think. It all depends on who or what we're allowing to define perfection. Perhaps we're just unaware of what we want, and we're defining perfection by the ideals of others instead of defining it for ourselves. My perfect life will be different from your perfect life. Knowing this will help to change our perspective. See beyond imperfections; you may just have a perfect view! Enjoy!

July 9

Good Morning Sunshine! Make it a day of Following the Example of Jesus Anyway! Did you ever have one of those days? You know what I'm talking about, one of those days where anything that could go wrong did go wrong, and you found yourself frustrated, angry, sad, overwhelmed, feeling alone and forgotten, and you just felt like crying or giving up? We've all had at least one of those days, maybe more. If crawling under a rock were possible, I'm sure we'd find ourselves in good company. If you haven't felt like this, good for you! But for the rest of us, I'd like to encourage you to follow the example of Jesus anyway! Hiding under a rock won't solve anything, but following Christ will! Jesus knows exactly how we feel. He's been there! He's been frustrated, angry, sad, and overwhelmed. He felt alone and forgotten, heartbroken, and He wept. Here's the cool thing, He followed God anyway! He kept moving forward, trusting in God. He never lost sight or focus of His mission and ministry. We're to do the same; follow the example of Jesus anyway in spite of our feelings! Stay focused, follow Jesus, and Enjoy!

July 10

Good Morning Sunshine! Make it a Day of Living in Light! That's much easier to do once spring arrives, isn't it? With the turning of clocks, we get extra daylight, and with summer approaching, our hours of light extend. We wear lighter clothing, walk a little lighter, and our attitudes seem brighter. It's as though the whole world embraces this new life and light, as it should. Light allows us to grow and thrive and to be out embracing the world around us, and it's amazing that we begin to see people again; walking, playing in the parks, exercising, and just be-ing because they're drawn to the light and the warmth. We base much of our life on the weather, and it's true that sunlight has a great effect on our mood, but Scripture tells us that Jesus is the Light of the world. As followers of Christ, we should be drawn to this light that allows us to grow and thrive and be out embracing the world around us! We are encouraged to be in the Light no matter the weather, and not only that, we are invited to BE the Light and draw others to Light! Live in Light, share light, be the Light and Enjoy!

July 11

Good Morning Sunshine! Make it a Day of Good Thinking! I read that you can't have a positive life with a negative mind. Well, I didn't need to read that to know it, and I'm sure you knew that already too. So then why do we forget what we know so often? Why is it that our moods, attitudes, and outlook fluctuate with the wind, and we allow people, situations, and circumstances to dictate or change our positive thoughts and steal away our joy? Proverbs 23:7 says: "For as he thinks in his heart, so is he." So, if we think positively in our hearts, we are positive. If we love in our hearts, we are love. If we think compassion, grace, mercy, or joy, we are compassion, grace, mercy, and joy. If we think the opposite, well, you get the picture, so quit thinking the opposite! No one's circumstances are ideal 100% of the time. It's not just you! However, you can choose your mood, attitude, and outlook. Even if you don't fully believe in your heart, you can speak positive words over and over again, and you can choose to live in joy until your heart and mind catch up to one another! Choose to have a good mood, a great attitude, and a positive outlook! Choose good thinking, and Enjoy!

July 12

Good Morning Sunshine! Make it a Day of Spending Wisely! Don't panic; I'm not talking about cash. We spend much more than money every single day. We spend our time, thoughts, energy, feelings, and emotions; we spend ourselves every day. The question is, are you spending you wisely? Are you spending time with people you love and making the most of every moment? You may not be doing your favorite things every moment of every day, but you can still spend your time making every moment count! Where are you spending your thoughts? Are you thinking of what is true and right and holy, and are you thinking of things or people that will benefit you and your life, those things that are healthy, or are your thoughts stuck in the past or thinking, I coulda, shoulda, woulda or of others who don't give you a second thought? Where are you spending your energy? Are you helping those in need or even yourself, or do you expend your energy complaining? How do you spend your feelings? Do you wallow in self-pity or pine over lost loves, dreams or goals, or do you feel determined to move beyond your circumstances? You only get to live today once. Spend YOU wisely, and Enjoy!

July 13

Good Morning Sunshine! Make it a Day of Living Fully in Spite of Your Fear! Every day we're hearing of tragic events, so much so that it has become almost commonplace. We're bombarded by news of natural disasters, violence exploding in the streets, shootings at malls, movie theaters, places of worship, and schools, and missing children, not to mention the sheer volume of division among us. Is there any place that's safe? Is there anywhere that we can go and not be afraid? If we look at this from the world's perspective, the answer would be a resounding "no." However, as children of God, the answer is much different! We can go everywhere because we have faith, hope, and trust in God. The world is scary, for sure, but we can turn to God to strengthen and guide us, to help us live, and live abundantly, to live fully, in spite of our fears. 2 Timothy 1:7 says: "For God has not given us a spirit of fear and timidity, but of power and of love and sound mind," John 14:27 says: "I am leaving you with a gift - peace of mind and heart. The peace I give is a gift the world cannot give. So don't be troubled or afraid," Psalm 112:7 says: "They do not fear bad news, they confidently trust the Lord to care for them." Don't succumb to the evils of this world, and don't be afraid to live confidently while holding fast to God. Pray for those who have been affected by the tragedy. Help others in the ways that only you can and in the ways God calls you to. But live by embracing your life fully in spite of your fears, and Enjoy!

July 14

Good Morning Sunshine! Make it a Day of Seeing Clearly! It is true that two people can look at the very same thing or witness the exact same event, yet they see it in completely different ways. It is all about perspective. Well, that is how it is with life as well. Everyone encounters difficult circumstances, yet some will see a way through and be determined to overcome the odds. Conversely, others won't allow themselves to see beyond the struggle. They allow their situations or challenges to overcome them. It comes down to our vision and, believe it or not, how we view ourselves. We often see the world, life, people, and circumstances, not as they are but more so the way we are. If we see ourselves as afraid, we will live in fear of taking chances, meeting new people, letting go of those things that are unnecessary, or living our lives fully. If we see ourselves as ugly, we will never see the beauty that surrounds us. If we see ourselves as weak, we will never gather the strength or courage to change and create the life we were meant to live. If we see only obstacles that hinder us from moving forward, we will never see challenges as the potential that can help us grow! Matthew 6:22 tells us: "The eye is the lamp of the body. If your eyes are healthy, your whole body will be full of light." See yourself and the world through the eyes of Christ today. See yourself as a precious, beloved, and beautiful child of God. If you see yourself that way, you will not only see yourself clearly, but you will also see the world in a much better light. Check your vision, see clearly and Enjoy!

July 15

Good Morning Sunshine! Make it a Day of Not Wishing Your Life Away! Do you ever notice that we are so busy anticipating what's coming next that we forget to embrace what we have right now? If you hate the cold of winter, you wish for spring, and if you love the beach, then you wish for summer. If you are in school, you wish for the end of the semester. If it is Monday, you wish it was Friday. We never seem to embrace the moment we are living in. Our eyes, minds, and hearts are always looking ahead. If we are always looking at the next month, day or moment, what happens to the month, day, or moment that we are living in right now? Then we look back and wonder how time could have gone by so quickly, not realizing that we wished for it, and we forgot to embrace so many of life's moments. Take today slowly, no matter what the day brings. Take each moment as it comes and embrace it. Take the time to engage others; talk, laugh, listen and embrace relationships, creation, and the world around you. Breathe deeply, take in your surroundings, capture the moment, live fully in it, and Enjoy!

July 16

Good Morning Sunshine! Make it a Day of Being a Peacemaker! Matthew 5:9 says: "Blessed are the peacemakers for they will be called children of God." When, not if, conflict comes your way, how do you handle it? Do you get angry, scream, shout, cry, stomp your feet, throw things, pout? Not everything will go your way every day. You will not necessarily like every person or situation you encounter. As children of God, we are to choose peace, not only because it is better than other options, like lashing out in anger or seeking revenge. Rather, we choose peace because of who we are, children of God. Anyone can yell; it takes strength to listen, hold your tongue, and speak in love and in spirit and truth. We are to be peacemakers, not anger provokers. We are to bring harmony during the conflict, listening, embracing, and engaging others. As peacemakers, we communicate feelings and thoughts in responsible ways. Be creative, get to the heart of any situation, and seek to transform it into something new. As children of God, be the presence of God. Live out the peace that God offers. Speak kindness, Live in love and joy. Be a peacemaker, and Enjoy!

July 17

Good Morning Sunshine! Make it a Day of Being You! Did you ever take notice of the people around you and wish that you could be more like them? I wish I looked like them. I wish I had their talent. I wish I had their job, education, intelligence, stuff, etc. We do it all the time, and for whatever reason, we somehow start to believe that we are not good enough because we are not like so and so. We begin to lose confidence in ourselves and allow self-doubt and self-condemnation to creep in. We forget that we are unique creations of God, and we each have a unique meaning and purpose. It's great to admire the gifts and talents of another, and it's great to learn from others, but if we're so focused on what they have and what we think we're lacking, we may never discover our own beauty, gifts, and talents. Romans 12:6 says that we all have different gifts that God has given us, and we're to use them. We can't use our gifts if we're looking at someone else's. Oscar Wilde said: "Be yourself; everyone else is taken." Be YOU today! YOUR gifts, YOUR talents, and YOUR life makes a difference! BE YOU and Enjoy!!

July 18

Good Morning Sunshine! Make it a Day of Fighting the Good Fight of Faith! 1 Timothy 6:12 says: "Fight the good fight for what we believe. Hold tightly to the eternal life that God has given you." What we often forget is that everything is temporary, everything but God and God's promises to us, that is. Our current circumstances and struggles won't last forever; they're temporary. Yet, while we are facing these things or situations, they may seem like they'll go on forever, and there's no escape. We often feel like giving up, giving in, and waving our white flag in surrender, and there are times that we don't feel like fighting the good fight. The truth is that we forget in the span of our life these situations are momentary, but God's love, God's presence, and God's promises are eternal. Life changes constantly; nothing stays the same. In the midst of the temporary, hold fast to what is eternal. Draw from God to strengthen your faith, your courage, and your tenacity, and use this in your life and in your circumstances to persevere. You can do it! Don't fear temporary; rejoice in eternal! Fight the good fight of faith, and Enjoy!

July 19

Good Morning Sunshine! Make it a Christ-Centered Day! I don't know about you, but it seems most days are centered on everything but Christ. Our days are centered on how we feel, our busy schedules, work, home, school, family and friends, and our circumstances. If we think of it before meals, we might bring Jesus in while we say a quick prayer, and if there is the time at the end of the day, while we are lying in bed, we might begin saying a prayer, yawn, to give God thanks....zzzzzz. Then we wake up and begin again. In the fast-paced world we live in, it is easy to lose our focus and get caught up in things and stuff. We lose sight of Christ, and before we know it, life seems unbalanced, and we are so distracted as everything is vying for our attention. We attempt to attend to every little fleeting thing while losing focus of the One thing that is everlasting and will sustain us, Jesus. There is a certain peace that comes when Christ is our center. Center your thoughts, words, and deeds on Christ today. Breathe in peace, live in joy, love, laugh, and focus on what is most important, Christ and Enjoy!

July 20

Good Morning Sunshine! Make it a Day of Cleaning Up! Did you ever notice that we hang onto stuff? Yes, physical stuff, but we also clutter our minds with negative thoughts and feelings of anger, loneliness, unforgiveness, pain, hurt, etc. We hang onto the past, wishing we could relive it because it was so much better "when," or we live with regret and can't let it go and move forward. We hold fast to people and relationships that are unhealthy because we think we can change others to be what we want them to be, or we would rather have a bad relationship than no relationship. We have become hoarders! However, what we are stockpiling is all these unnecessary things. We are being overtaken from within. Our spirits, our minds, and our hearts are buried under so much "stuff!" It is time to clean up whatever it is that is cluttering our heart, mind, and soul! God does something new every day, but if we are too busy trying to just get through all of this other "stuff," how can we make room for new blessings and opportunities? 2 Corinthians 5:17 says: "If anyone is in Christ, there is a new creation. The old is gone; the new has come." Clean up, let go and be open to new blessings and Enjoy!

July 21

Good Morning Sunshine! Make it a Day of Walking with Your Head Held High! Much can be said about the way a person carries themselves. Those with confidence, or the lack of confidence, are evident in the walk. Those who are confident have shoulders back and hold their heads up high and walk with purpose. Those who lack confidence are quite the opposite. Happy people smile and walk a little lighter, maybe even with a bounce in their step, much more so than those who carry burdens; their steps are a little heavier. Now I understand that some may be hurting inside and have less than ideal circumstances, but even with life's challenges, some choose to walk with a sense of purpose anyway, as if to say: "I'm trying, and I refuse to give in or succumb to my feelings." While for others, it is plain to see they feel defeated and have given up, and it is on display for all to see. How are you walking today? What can others determine about you by the way you carry yourself? Let me remind you that you are a child of God and that alone should help you to walk with your head a little higher. Does your walk say I am loved, I am beautiful, and I belong to Christ? It should, because you are loved, you are beautiful, and you do belong to Christ. Be confident in who you are and to whom you belong! Hold your head up high and Enjoy!

July 22

Good Morning Sunshine! Make it a Day of Running the Race! Did you ever have one of those days where you just felt like throwing your hands up in the air, stopping in your tracks, and just quitting or giving up? Maybe you have had a bad day at work, you are in a difficult relationship, or experiencing the frustration that life seems to be bombarding you with, one challenge after another, the news and social media are too much to bear? It is true that life is not always easy, nor are circumstances always ideal. However, life itself is always beautiful and always worth celebrating. We just need to choose to see the beauty and the small moments that are worth celebrating. We need to continue to move forward, run the race, and make it to the finish line! Martin Luther King, Jr. said: "If you can't fly, then run. If you can't run, then walk; if you can't walk, then crawl, but whatever you do, you have to keep moving forward." What he was saying is, don't stop, don't give up, don't give in, keep going and finish the race! 1 Corinthians 9:24 says: "Do you not know that in a race all runners compete, but only one receives the prize. Run in such a way that you may win it." Keep running the race and only throw your hands up to praise God, give thanks for all of your beautiful blessings, and cross the finish line in victory and celebration! Run the Race and Enjoy!

July 23

Good Morning Sunshine! Make it a Day of Seeing the Good! Did you ever notice how easy it is to see the bad, to pick out flaws, point out mistakes and what we believe is wrong? We do it to others, to ourselves, and to our surroundings. Then, oddly enough, we wonder why we are not happy, why we live with negative thoughts and why things, why life, can't be better. Here's the thing, you will see exactly what you are looking for! If you look for kindness, you will see it. If you look for beauty, you will see it. If you look for love and generosity, you will see it. Once you see it, suddenly, before you know it, you will start living it! You might find that you see happiness in your life and goodness in others around you! If your vision is telling you otherwise, look in a new direction, look in a new place or choose to see what's already around you with a new attitude! If you can't see the goodness around you, perhaps you need to take a deeper look within you. Matthew 6:22 says: "The eyes are like a lamp for the body. If your eyes are sound, your whole body will be full of light." See the goodness life has to offer, be filled with light, and Enjoy!

July 24

Good Morning Sunshine! Make it a Rich day!! We associate being rich with our wallet or bank account, with money and financial prosperity. We have all been asked the question, "What would you do if you had a million dollars?" And dreaming about it is fun. Rich, by definition, is having wealth or great possessions, abundantly supplied with resources of great worth or value. There are no dollar signs in this definition; it has become what we have made it, about money. However, let me share some great news ~ YOU ARE RICH!! Most things in the life of true worth and value don't come with a dollar sign! You may be struggling financially, but if you have family and friends to love and they love you in return, you have great wealth! If you have strong character and integrity, faith and hope, you have valuable resources that many are lacking. Peace of mind can't be bought. If you woke up this morning and are breathing, you are wealthy beyond compare, and this day holds an abundance of rich blessings if you are willing to recognize them. YOU have great worth and value by virtue of being alive! YOU are so Rich! Live like it and Enjoy!

July 25

Good Morning Sunshine! Make it a Day of Being in Conversation with God! Do you ever make an effort to communicate with God? Do you make prayer part of your daily routine? Prayer itself is just talking to God. We might pray at mealtimes and at bedtime and if we have a crisis, but do you take the time to pray when things are going well or to give thanks. Do you pray with and for others? Do you talk to or spend time with God to maintain or strengthen your relationship with God and with others? Do you pray wherever you are, or do you wait until you are in the proper position, on your knees with your hands folded perfectly with just the right lighting, when no one else is around? If we wait for ideal circumstances, we will pray very little. Victor Hugo said: "Certain thoughts are prayers. There are moments when whatever be the attitude of the body, the soul is on its knees." And 1 Thessalonians 5:17 says: "Pray without ceasing." We can't spend our lives in this 'proper' praying position, but we can be in constant communication with God in our hearts and minds and from the depths of our souls. Converse with God, be strengthened, and Enjoy!

July 26

Good Morning Sunshine! Make it a Day of Choice! Do you realize the amazing options that are waiting for you to choose today? There are so many. The possibilities are endless! You get to choose to make this a good day, a bad day, or even a fantastic day! You can choose to smile and rise above circumstances. You can choose your friends, and You can choose who you love. If they don't reciprocate, you can choose to wallow or move forward and find new friends and new loves. You can choose your attitude, negative or positive. You can choose what, or whom, to believe. You can choose right from wrong, to love or hate, to sing or be silent, to walk or run, to be transformed, or to remain the same. You have the choice to live or just merely exist. The point is that you have the gift of choice. Life will continue to provide options, but you have to make the choice, to try or not. You can choose to believe God has a plan for you and do all you can to follow it or not. My hope is that you will choose to live today to its fullest and choose to make it the best day ever until tomorrow! Make the choice and Enjoy!

July 27

Good Morning Sunshine! Make it a Nothing's Impossible Day!! If you counted all the times you had a task before you or an idea come to mind, and you dismissed them with thoughts of "I can't," how many tick marks would you have written down? There are many times in life that we are limited in possibilities by our own self-doubt and lack of confidence. There are so many times things were impossible simply because we thought it to be and made it a reality. What if you thought differently today? What if you believed in the impossible? What if you believed you could do, be, or accomplish anything? What if you believed your contributions to the world could have a far-reaching impact and make a difference? We often see defeat before we even get started, so we never try. Scripture tells us that all things are possible with God. What if you really believed that to be true? What if you made a decision today that, instead of believing in impossibilities, you ask yourself, how can this situation, circumstance, or challenge become possible? If you believe, then the possibilities are endless! Trust God and believe that it, whatever it is, is possible! Believe and Enjoy!

July 28

Good Morning Sunshine! Make it a Day of Looking Lovely! Roald Dahl said, "If you have good thoughts, they will shine out of your face like sunbeams, and you will always look lovely." Wouldn't it be awesome if you shined great light that attracted others, and with just your thoughts alone, you would radiate a brightness that lit the way for others to follow. How great it would be to think good thoughts and look lovely! If you knew that others could see your thoughts through your face, what would they see right now? What would your thoughts say about you? Would they say I choose to live in joy despite my circumstances, or I choose to allow my circumstances to overshadow my joy? Would you shine brightly or be void of light? If you are not shining, what you need to remember is that your thoughts belong to you. What that means is you can choose to think anything you want! No one can make you think negative thoughts; though some may try, you have a choice to allow it to happen or not! Don't allow anyone or anything to steal your joy and hijack your thoughts! Philippians 4:8 says: "Whatever is true, whatever is honorable, whatever is just, whatever is pure, whatever is lovely, whatever is commendable if there is any excellence, if there is anything worthy of praise, think about these things." Think good thoughts today, my friends! Shine brightly, look lovely and Enjoy!

July 29

Good Morning Sunshine! Make it a Day of Eye Contact! Did you ever think about eye contact before? We don't often think of it, and during the busyness of our days, we don't often do it. We pass people saying hello or how are you while still in motion with nothing more than a quick glance and many times with the hope that they won't answer. What if you made eye contact and slowed down and said hello and asked how are you while standing still and really meant it as a question and waited for an answer? I understand the hectic nature of our lives, but we were created to be in a relationship with one another, to journey together, to encourage, support, care for, and love one another. That's not so easy to do when we don't even take the time to look at each other. Hebrew 10:24-25 says: "Let us think of ways to motivate one another to acts of love and good works. And let us not neglect our meeting together, as some people do, but encourage one another." We sometimes neglect to see how blessed we are simply by the people that we get to share life with. Make eye contact today, see the blessings, gifts, and love before you and Enjoy!

July 30

Good Morning Sunshine! Make it a Day of Walking on Holy Ground! Did you realize that Holy Ground is not just in a church or sanctuary? Holy ground is wherever the presence of God is. In John 17:23, as Jesus is praying to God, He says: "I am in them, and you are in me. May they experience such perfect unity that the world will know that you sent me and that you love them as much as you love me." The Spirit of God lives and dwells within us. We are loved with a perfect and Holy love that lives and dwells inside of us. Every time we share the love of God, we are standing on Holy Ground. When you reach out in love to help someone in need, whether you supply physical or material sustenance or offer words of kindness and compassion, or you encourage or support another, you are standing on Holy Ground. When you recognize God in all creation, nature, or in humanity, you are standing on Holy Ground. When you lift up, build up or speak up or speak out for social justice, you are standing on Holy Ground. When you choose right from wrong, you are standing on Holy Ground. When you follow the will of God rather than the will of the world, you are standing on Holy Ground. When you feed the hungry, clothe the poor, visit the sick, and you love your neighbor, all of your neighbors, you are standing on Holy Ground. When you offer or receive forgiveness or extend the grace of God, you are standing on Holy Ground. When you see beyond your circumstances and choose to live in faith and joy and have a peace that passes all understanding, you are standing on Holy Ground. May God be with you today, and may you recognize that the ground you walk on is Holy because God is with you. Walk on Holy Ground and Enjoy!

July 31

Good Morning Sunshine! Make it a Day of Being a Genius! Don't scoff; YOU are a Genius!! Albert Einstein said: "Everybody is a genius. But if you judge a fish by its ability to climb a tree, it will spend its whole life believing that it is stupid." We judge everyone, especially ourselves. We are quick to compare others to the way we are and find that we are frustrated when people don't think, act or perform like we do. Basically, we judge the fish because it can't climb a tree. Then the rest of the time, we're so busy trying to be like someone else, comparing ourselves, and attempting to become the type of "genius" they are that we spend way too much time and energy on being the fish trying to climb the tree and feeling stupid. Teach people what you know, but love and accept them for who they are. Learn all you can from those around you and allow yourself to gain knowledge to become all you have been created to be. However, remember we are all genius in our own way. We are all beautiful creations and children of God. Be your own genius, and Enjoy!

August

August 1

Good Morning Sunshine! Make it a day of Compliments! I have heard human nature tends to complain loudly and compliment softly. This is so true. We tend to be very quick to express our displeasure, our anger, and frustration. When we are not happy, the world seems to know it. We raise our voices and show it by the expression on our faces. We tell people they are wrong, or we let them know they haven't done something to our liking without a second thought. I am not suggesting that we do not express ourselves, but that we examine how we share it. And perhaps give some thought to this: does the world know when we are happy when we like something or someone? Do we pay compliments or lift others up as easily as we complain or bring them down? 1 Thessalonians 5:11 says: "Therefore encourage one another and build each other up." Ephesians 4:29 says: "Don't use foul or abusive language. Let everything you say be good and helpful so that your words will be an encouragement to those who hear them." Use your voice to encourage others and lift them up. Express your compliments loudly and your complaints softly, and Enjoy!

August 2

Good Morning Sunshine! Make it a Day of "But Wait There's More!" You have heard the late-night infomercials; just when you are ready to turn the channel, you hear the famous words, "but wait, there's more," and so you hold out and watch just a little longer to see the offer and if it is worth it. What if we used this same concept for life and with our faith? What if we believe there was more than what we can possibly know at any given moment, and we hold out believing it is true? Our struggles often cloud the idea that there is anything else waiting for us or that life has more to offer. When finances are tight, our focus is money - God tells us, but wait, there's more - I can provide you with everything money can't buy; love, peace, and joy. When your relationships are broken and your heart is pained, God says, but wait, there's more – I am near to the brokenhearted, and I save the crushed in spirit, I heal and bind up wounds (Psalm 34:18, 147:3). When everything that could go wrong does, God says, but wait, there's more; No, despite these things, overwhelming victory is ours through Christ who loves us! (Romans 8:37). See what's beyond circumstances, wait for the offer, and trust God; there's more! Enjoy!

August 3

Good Morning Sunshine! Make it an Unacceptable Day!! Did you ever notice that we just accept whatever the day brings? If we are happy, we embrace the day. Who wouldn't love a happy day? We will take it if life gives it to us! The question is, why are we waiting for life to give it to us? That is unacceptable! On the flip side, if things are just status quo and they don't go our way or life seems too difficult, we might get mad, wallow and complain, but we just take it for what it is; we accept it. My life is boring, nothing ever goes my way, or life's a b%$#& and then you die. That is accepting a life of mediocrity, misery, and drama. That is unacceptable. So, why do we do it? I don't know about you, but I don't believe God created us to just take life as it comes. That, to me, is unacceptable! I believe we are created to make something out of life for ourselves and those around us. We are to live fully because we are children of God. Life will hand us a raw deal many times, but it is up to us to accept it or refuse it! God always offers us hope and joy, and that, too, is up to us to accept it or refuse it. You want to be happy? Choose it! Choose to live in joy despite your circumstances! Anything less than living a life of love, hope, peace, and joy as a child of God is unacceptable! Go live the way God wants you to live and Enjoy!

August 4

Good Morning Sunshine! Make it a Day of Practicing Hope! Norman Vincent Peale said, "Practice hope. As hopefulness becomes a habit, you can achieve a permanently happy spirit." Can you imagine having a permanently happy spirit? Can we handle a permanently happy spirit? This may mean smiling more often than not, being optimistic in every situation, and working to find solutions. A happy spirit means you believe that there are better things to come and see good in the people and the world around you. A happy spirit may mean forgiving those who hurt you the most, not for them but for your own happiness and peace of mind. It may mean that you laugh in spite of the pain and that you cry while persevering, never giving up, and continuing to move forward. A happy spirit may mean that you think of others before you think of yourself, and crazy enough, you want to reach out to help others obtain a happy spirit too. A happy spirit may mean you strive to be your best in all things. The only way to find out if a permanently happy spirit is possible is to practice hope until it becomes a habit! Get practicing and Enjoy!

August 5

Good Morning Sunshine! Make it a Day to Keep Going! Sometimes that's easier said than done. Sometimes life events stop you in your tracks. Sometimes we wonder if it's worth it to keep going because it seems as though we're moving, but the journey is always uphill or filled with obstacles. Andy Warhol said: "It does not matter how slowly you go so long as you do not stop." We all feel like 'stopping' every now and then along the way to catch our breath, to see things from a new or different perspective, but the key is to keep moving. Psalm 18:32 says: "It is God who arms me with strength and makes my way perfect." If we believe God is with us, arming us with strength, then we must believe that our way can be perfected with trust, faith, hope, determination, and perseverance. I understand that none of those are easy, but each will sustain us to keep moving and get to the top of the hill or over hurdles or thwart obstacles. Our goal is to keep moving and not allow anything to stop us. Some days we'll run. Other days we'll crawl. Be determined to keep going and Enjoy!

August 6

Good Morning Sunshine! Make it a Day of Being Hope! Every day there are tragic events that unfold around us. These circumstances and crises create in us heavy hearts and cause the light we once saw to become dim. Charles Spurgeon said: "Hope itself is like a star, not to be seen in the sunshine of prosperity, and only to be discovered in the night of adversity." Having hope never promises that we are guaranteed anything. Having hope is the glimmer of light that says there are possibilities, and it's the hope of all things possible that keeps us going. We are hope, and it is up to us to keep the glimmer of light shining in the darkness for others to see. If you pray, you have hope, and you are hope. If you reach out to help others, you have hope, and you are hope. If you love, stand firm in the face of adversity, if you laugh in spite of it all, if you see possibilities, then you have hope, and you are hope. The world needs hope! If you have hope and you are hope, then the world needs you! Have hope today! Share hope and be hope and light the way for others. Enjoy!

August 7

Good Morning Sunshine! Make it a Day of Using Your Life! We have been given the gift of life. Some of us have more earthly time than others, but we all have the option of what to do with our lives, and we need to use it while we can, today, now. Tomorrow is not guaranteed. So, are you using your life or just letting it slowly slip away? Are you using the love in your heart to love others deeply? Are you using it by giving it away? Are you using your time to be a presence, a listening ear, a helping hand, an encouraging supporter, and a compassionate friend? Are you using your resources to make a difference in the lives of others, to make the world, or at least your small section of it, a better place? The purpose of life is to use it and to live it fully, and to share it. Your life is a gift to you and to others. 1 Peter 4:10 says: "God has given each of you a gift from his great variety of spiritual gifts. Use them well to serve one another." We have one life to live, one life to use. How are you using your life? Are you using your life? Use your life by living it fully. Use your life by sharing it. Use your life by contributing to the goodness of the world. Use your life and Enjoy!

August 8

Good Morning Sunshine! Make it a Day of Forgetting! Remember yesterday and last week and last year and many years ago? Of course, we do. We remember what was or how we wish things had been different. We look back with coulda, shoulda, woulda thoughts, and if only I knew then what I know now. Well, sometimes we can learn from those thoughts and memories, but often we get stuck there. We can't go back to yesterday, and we can't change or un-change anything prior to this very moment and what happens today and tomorrow. More often than not, we need to forget about all of our yesterdays so we can live in our todays. We don't need to let go of our cherished memories of family and friends and experiences that remind us of life's blessings, but more often, we hang onto mistakes and regret like they're dear friends. Crazy thought, but yesterday's regrets are not thinking about us at all; why is it we can't forget about them? Isaiah 43:18 says: "Remember not the former things, nor consider the things of old." We can't undo the past, but we can choose to forget it, to let go, to move on, and live today! Forget and Enjoy!

August 9

Good Morning Sunshine! Make it a Day of Finding Remedies! A remedy, by definition, is something that cures, heals, or relieves. A remedy restores natural or proper conditions or removes an evil of any kind. Henry Ford said: "Don't find fault, find a remedy; anybody can complain." Have you noticed we complain a lot? We don't like this; we think that's wrong, it doesn't look right, taste right, feel right, they should have done it this way, that way, my way. Our list of complaints is long. If we don't like something, we complain first and usually continue complaining rather than seeking a resolution or a remedy. What if we, instead of complaining, used the energy we expend in fault finding, moaning, or groaning, to actually working to find a remedy or a way to cure, heal or relieve whatever it is that we're complaining about? What if we took the time to invest in making a difference, changing things for the better or listening to, getting to know, or opening our hearts to other people so we could gain better understanding? Perhaps that's the ultimate remedy, doing our part to make changes rather than just voicing our opinion. Don't like something? Find remedies, be the difference and Enjoy!

August 10

Good Morning Sunshine! Make it a Day of Being in a Good Mood! The thing about your mood is that you can determine what it is, good, bad, happy, miserable, loving, angry, etc. There are many external forces that can affect your mood, but you get to decide whether to allow it to happen or not! Your mood will determine many things; how you relate to others, how they relate or don't relate to you, and your outlook on life, people, and the world around you. You know what I mean. You can spot a bad mood a mile away, and it makes you want to run in the opposite direction. Nothing about a bad mood or having a bad attitude is inviting. We want to avoid it at all costs. However, if you are in a good mood and have a positive attitude, then others are drawn to you and you to them. There is a great spirit and energy that attracts us to those who are happy, and then we get caught up in it, or others catch what we are giving out. Psalm 144:15 says: "Yes, joyful are those who live like this! Joyful indeed are those whose God is the Lord." And, as followers of Christ, we are to live in joy and peace, having faith, hope, and trust in God. You are not demonstrating that in a bad mood. Choose your mood. Make it good and Enjoy!

August 11

Good Morning Sunshine! Make it a Day of Not Settling! We somehow have become satisfied with less than. We settle in many aspects of our lives, not realizing that every one of us has the potential for greatness!! Yes, YOU have the potential for greatness! We settle for only living a partial or mediocre life, and we don't even know it. Remember being a kid and having amazing dreams and desires of what we were going to accomplish in life? Somewhere along the line, some of us began to settle for less, and our dreams and desires became smaller or non-existent. We have settled for the ordinary and routine, and we have stopped going the extra mile. We have settled for less for ourselves and others around us and have become comfortable in it. What areas of your life have you settled? Settling for less means accepting less than you truly deserve. Jesus said in John 10:10 that he came that we might have a rich and satisfying life, a full life, a life of abundance. But we need to know that the thing with not settling is that work, determination, perseverance, faith, and risking pain are involved. I think we know this, so we sometimes settle out of fear of these things. I encourage you to dream again, to set goals and to have visions and to go after them, knowing that God doesn't want you to settle but to live your life to its fullest. Don't settle. Strive for the abundant life God desires for you, and Enjoy!

August 12

Good Morning Sunshine! Make it a day of Restarting! Every once in a while, my laptop will give me a notice of new updates that will allow my computer programs to have the most current information and work more efficiently. In order to implement the new programs or the new way of doing things, I need to restart the laptop. I do, and things work well. Dare I say they even run smoothly. Strangely enough, it reminds me of life. Every day we are given new information, we gain knowledge and learn what to do and what not to do, and sometimes changes or updates to our current "programs" can allow our lives to be more efficient and run more smoothly. This also happens in our spiritual life when we realize that a life in Christ will restart who we are, and we are reminded to whom we belong. 2 Corinthians 5:17 says: "This means that anyone who belongs to Christ has become a new person. The old life is gone; a new life has begun!" Updating, re-thinking, and restarting with new knowledge, new information, and a new or renewed faith can change our outlook and can allow our days and our lives to go more smoothly. If we are doing things right, then, we are constantly learning and installing new information that can help us make better decisions, and that will assist in living fuller, happier lives. We are to take that information and restart our way of thinking and living. Update your life as much as possible, refresh, renew, restart and Enjoy!

August 13

Good Morning Sunshine! Make it a Day of Being "That" Person! I know, I know, we have all been to parties where "that" person has been loud and obnoxious. We have been in stores and restaurants and witnessed "that" person' complaining loudly, being rude, or talking down to others. Usually, nobody wants to be "that" person, whew!! The thing is, we remember "that" person, and we talk about "that" person, sharing their antics and poor behavior in stories to others. What if you could change "that" person into a good thing? What if you were "that" person who used your unique gifts and talents or your resources to touch the lives of others in a positive way. What if you were "that" person who spoke words of kindness and compassion? What if you were "that" person to be the voice of hope or encouragement in a bleak situation. What if you were "that" person who lived your life to make a difference and impact the world in a positive way. Here's the thing - it only takes one person to change the world, to overcome the odds, to see the light in the darkness, to live as an example for others to follow. You can be "that" person if you choose to be. So what's stopping you? Be "that" person, make a positive difference and Enjoy!

August 14

Good Morning Sunshine! Make it a Day of Being Courageous! You may not think you need to be courageous to get through today or most of your days, but I believe living life takes courage. It takes courage to be happy when your circumstances tell you to be miserable. It takes courage to love because you are risking pain and grief if relationships end in any manner; breaks-ups, fallouts, moving, or the passing of a loved one. It takes courage to think for yourself but more courage to share those thoughts with others. It takes courage to know what you want out of life and to pursue your dreams and goals without giving up in difficult moments. It takes courage to stand firm in your beliefs when others disagree with you. It takes courage to give your resources away to help someone else when your resources are limited. It takes courage to be yourself when you are not exactly who the world wants you to be. It takes courage to challenge yourself to not just be who you are today but rather be open to becoming all God has created you to be. Joshua 1:9 says: "Be strong and courageous. Do not fear, do not be discouraged. The Lord, your God will be with you, wherever you go." Life takes courage! Be Courageous and Enjoy!

August 15

Good Morning Sunshine! Make it a Day of Not Forgetting the Errand! Huh? In a nutshell, it means don't forget your mission in life. Woodrow Wilson said: "You are not here merely to make a living. You are here in order to enable the world to live more amply, with greater vision, with a finer spirit of hope and achievement. You are here to enrich the world, and you impoverish yourself if you forget the errand." If you want to live a rich life, this is the formula. You are here to make a difference, to touch the lives of others, to leave your mark on the world, one person, one achievement, one kind gesture at a time. If you want to be a person who has great wealth, live your life for others. Your bank account won't change (sorry), but your heart and your life will. Show the world God's creation in you by living out this calling, your errand, to demonstrate the greatest commandments, to love God with all your heart, mind, and strength, and by loving your neighbor as yourself. Help others to live more amply, with greater vision, and with a spirit of hope! Don't forget the errand, and Enjoy!

August 16

Good Morning Sunshine! Make it a Day of Not Being Salty! In the Book of Genesis, God told Abraham to leave behind everything he knew to go to an unknown place and life. Abraham had faith and trusted God. Long story short (please read Genesis), Abraham asked God if his nephew Lot could go as well, God said yes. So, Lot and his wife were leaving Sodom & Gomorrah, but Lot's wife kept looking behind her; she couldn't let go of the past. She had no idea what was waiting for her if she just let go and moved forward. She became a pillar of salt. Essentially, she became useless. Did you ever put too much salt on your food? A little salt tastes awesome, but a lot of salt will make food inedible. Well, I am encouraging you not to become too salty! We look back at woulda, coulda, shoulda, and lots of if onlys, but the truth is we can't change the past; we can only learn from it. And the old saying you don't know what you got 'til it's gone is true, but it's also true you don't know what's coming until it arrives. You can't see what's coming if you're only looking back! Trust and have faith in God; look ahead! Don't be Salty and Enjoy!

August 17

Good Morning Sunshine! Make it a Day of Loving You! Why is it we can love God, love others, love things, love food, places, and even television shows, but we have great trouble loving ourselves? We often believe everything in this world has value and worth, except for us. We wait for compliments to make us feel good or words of praise to say we're doing a good job, and if they don't come, we begin listening to our own negative thoughts, and we put ourselves down. Believe me; there are many who will do that for you, you shouldn't do it to yourself, or you will doubt your own abilities, lack self-confidence, and self-worth, and value yourself less and less. Let me remind you that YOU are a beautiful creation of God...YES, YOU!! We are commanded to love God, love others, AND to love ourselves. I'm fairly certain that loving you is a significant part of life and faith, so much so that it was specifically mentioned by Jesus Himself as part of the second greatest commandment. Do you see the irony here? You can't fully love others to the best of your ability unless you love yourself to the best of your ability. Love God, love others, and make it a priority to love you today and Enjoy!

August 18

Good Morning Sunshine! Make it a Day of Greeting Everyone with a Smile! Mother Teresa said: "Let us always meet each other with a smile, for the smile is the beginning of love." It seems such a simple act to share a smile, yet how often do we actually smile at one another? In my own experience, not nearly enough. Perhaps we don't truly recognize the power of a smile. A smile can be the beginning of love. But it can also express kindness, compassion, joy, and enthusiasm. Smiles can be contagious. Rarely have I smiled at someone, and they've not smiled back. We should be so contagious! If you think about every person you encounter on any given day, then you realize that they, like you, have experienced some sort of pain and suffering. Every person has experienced loss, and everyone struggles with something; no one is immune. So why wouldn't we want to share kindness, compassion, love, and joy whenever possible? You don't need to know the person you're smiling at to impact their day and to share the gift of love and kindness. You don't need to say a word. Just Smile and Enjoy

August 19

Good Morning Sunshine! Make it a Day of Leaving Everything A Little Better Than the Way You Found It! Did you ever go for a walk and see some sort of litter, and you took the time to pick it up rather than just walking by because *you* didn't put it there? Have you ever consoled someone who was hurting or helped to calm someone who was angry, or shared laughter during a conversation? Did you ever use your gifts, talents, and resources to teach someone or to benefit others? Did you ever change or grow from challenges and difficult situations that you faced and overcame? Did you ever take an old or used object that was discarded and unusable and restore it into something that looks brand new and now has a brand-new purpose? Well, what you've done is left something or someone, maybe even yourself, better than you found it/them/you. This should be how we live every day, doing all we can to make the world, our relationships, and our lives better than the way we found them. You have the opportunity to approach life with a positive attitude and to make this day, the world, others, and yourself better. Do it! Live by leaving everything a little better, and Enjoy!

August 20

Good Morning Sunshine! Make it a Day of Making the Pieces Fit! Did you ever spend hours putting a puzzle together only to find you're missing pieces? So frustrating! Life is sort of like a puzzle. We think we have all the pieces, but we take a step back and realize when we thought we had all we needed for a great life, pieces seem to be missing, and it doesn't quite match the picture we had in mind. Relationships change, and we lose people we love. We change jobs and move to new locations. Illness moves in, and financial difficulties weigh us down. We endure heartache, heartbreak, pain, and suffering. All the things that don't make our picture-perfect puzzle come together. The thing about our own life puzzle is that we get to fill the missing spaces and rearrange them to make everything fit. It's not always easy because life's puzzle is constantly changing, yet it always has the potential to come together beautifully in the end. The pieces never go back the same way twice, but we can choose how to fill the missing spaces. Love, laughter, faith, and hope are great space fillers. Choose them to complete your puzzle, and Enjoy!

August 21

Good Morning Sunshine! Make it a Day of Listening to Your Heart! We listen to the TV, radio, social media, and noise all around us. We listen to the advice of others, sometimes taking it, sometimes not. We listen to the opinions and judgments of others, usually accepting them, whether they're true or not, and take them to heart. But how often do we listen to our own hearts and take the time to reflect on how we feel and what we think or believe deep within without hearing everything or everyone else around us? Paul Coelho wrote: "You will never be able to escape your heart. So it's better to listen to what it has to say." Our hearts often know the answers to questions, yet we seek others for validation of what we already know. Our hearts always know right from wrong, yet we often ignore it and make poor choices. We give our hearts to those we love. We put our heart and soul into the work we do or the goals we strive to achieve. We wear our hearts on our sleeves. Your heart determines so much of your life and your choices. Take time to listen to what your heart is saying, and Enjoy!

August 22

Good Morning Sunshine! Make it a Day of Becoming More Than! We go through much of our lives convincing ourselves we are less than, weaker than, dumber than, poorer than. Why do we do that to ourselves? We are amazing and beautiful creations of God, but we forget our strength, we forget our potential, and we forget our intelligence. We look in the mirror, and somehow, we have amnesia about who created us. We rarely see our uniqueness and how special we are. And rather than seeing the beauty of God's creation looking back at us, we see what the world, not God or those who truly love and care for us, believe us to be. We are always on the cusp of unleashing our greatest self, yet we are our own worst enemy, binding ourselves to "less than" thinking. Let me remind you to whom you belong; YOU ARE A CHILD OF GOD! You are so much more than you think! You are stronger than you think. More intelligent than you think. You are so much more beautiful than you think! Allow yourself to become your greatest self. Start thinking "More Than" and become "More Than" and Enjoy!

August 23

Good Morning Sunshine! Make it a Day of Breathing Life Into…! Did you ever start a project or have a task before you and think it was almost impossible to complete before you even began? Then you decided to focus, set your mind and heart to it, and before you knew it, it was finished. What happened is that you were determined to pay attention, and, believe it or not, you gave it life. When we begin to pay attention, really pay attention, to projects, tasks, circumstances, and especially our relationships, we can breathe life into them. Steve Maraboli said: "Beautiful things happen when we pay attention to each other. By participating in your relationships, you breathe life into them." I couldn't agree more, but I would add a little more to that. Beautiful things happen when you pay attention to not only your relationships but your very life. Beautiful things happen when you participate in your life, invest in yourself and become enthusiastic about living. Job 33:4 says: "The Spirit of God made me what I am, the breath of God Almighty gave me life!" With the life and breath God gave you, YOU need to breathe life into it by participating, paying attention with your heart and mind, and having determination, hope, and enthusiasm. You may work at the same job, live with the same people, and go through the same daily routine, but when you begin to pay attention and participate with hope and enthusiasm, you breathe new life into everything! Breathe life into and Enjoy!

August 24

Good Morning Sunshine! Make it a White Hot Day! This has nothing to do with weather but everything to do with your spirit and your life. Roald Dahl wrote about living life with enthusiasm. He said if you're interested in something, "Embrace it with both arms, hug it, love it and be passionate about it. Lukewarm is no good. Hot is no good either. White Hot and passionate is the only thing to be." We tend to live lukewarm most of the time. We can take things or leave them. Lukewarm living leaves us in a state of indifference or apathy. Every once in a while, we get a little 'hotter' when a new opportunity or new relationships come along or when a burden is lifted or a blessing is received. This is often short-lived, and before we know it, we're lukewarm again. When was the last time you woke up enthusiastic about your day and ready to take it on with passion? Have you ever lived your life White Hot and Passionate? If so, good for you; share your enthusiasm and passion with others. If not, why not? Life is too short to be lukewarm! Embrace it with both arms, love it, hug it, and be passionate! Live White Hot and Enjoy!

August 25

Good Morning Sunshine! Make it a Day of Keeping No Record of Wrongs! We keep records of everything. Our closets and filing cabinets are full of records and important papers; taxes, business transactions, medical records, school report cards, kid's artwork, and memories that we have accumulated over the years. We keep records of the people we have encountered and places we have experienced with pictures and videos so we can hang onto good memories. We keep a record in our hearts and minds of those we love and care about. But somewhere within us, we also keep a record of those we don't necessarily like, and we keep records of those who have wronged us. 1 Corinthians 13:5 tells us that "love keeps no record of wrongs." To truly love, we need to let go of these records. Does this mean by letting go, we allow ourselves to be wronged again and again? Absolutely not! What it means is that by forgiving others, we can let go and move forward in our lives without negativity, anger, or even hatred filling our hearts and minds. Keeping no record of wrongs is about loving God and freeing ourselves. Clean out your 'I've been wronged' closets ~ love, live free, and Enjoy!

August 26

Good Morning Sunshine! Make it a Day of Immersion! A form of Baptism is immersion, where the whole body of a person is submerged in water. The actual definition of immersion is being deeply engaged or involved; absorption. What if we spent the day immersed? What if we were deeply engaged or involved in this day? Wouldn't it be great if we absorbed our surroundings and saw the beauty in the world around us? What if we were involved in relationships, investing our time in developing stronger relationships with those we love and care for, or in beginning new relationships? What if we were so deeply engaged or involved with God, so fully immersed, that we can only see love, in us, in others, and in the world. What if we absorbed this love and believed in God, who makes all things possible rather than our circumstances which often feel as if they overtake us. What if we were completely saturated from absorbing God that we splashed the gifts of peace, joy, hope, faith, mercy, forgiveness, grace, and love onto others simply by being ourselves? Live immersed rather than skimming the surface! Absorb God, splash love, and Enjoy!

August 27

Good Morning Sunshine! Make it a Day of Knowing Life is Good! I have seen the t-shirts and mugs telling me that "life is good." I have even seen spare tires on the back of jeeps sharing the message, "life is good!" Reminders are great, especially if circumstances are far from ideal, aren't they? Why is it we forget how good life can be when we experience difficulties or even if life just seems "normal," whatever that is? Psalm 118:24 says: "This is the day the Lord has made; let us rejoice and be glad in it." Why? Because Life is Good! God has given us life and breath and created others to share this life with so that we can love and be loved. God has surrounded us with the most beautiful creation to take in, to breathe in, and to remind us that life is good. Many will tell you the opposite because they can't see beyond circumstances, but life is always, always, always good! Circumstances may not be, but life itself is. Life is beautiful, precious, and far too short, and life is good. We should be living reminders to others of God's goodness and faithfulness. Our lives, our attitudes , and our actions, as children of God, should always shine the message that life is good! Know it, believe it, share it, and Enjoy!

August 28

Good Morning Sunshine! Make it a Day of Being Under the Influence! Now, normally, this would not be my recommendation because we naturally assume being under the influence is something negative. We all know when someone is under the influence of something unhealthy. However, in this case, what if we were under the influence of something positive and something that could affect the world around us and our own lives in a positive and beneficial way? What if we were under the influence of love or kindness or generosity? What if we were under the influence of doing the right thing and standing up for the right causes? What if we are under the influence of God and not the world? Mother Teresa said: "Put yourself under the influence of Jesus so that he may think his thoughts in your mind, do his work through your hands, for you will be all powerful with him to strengthen you." Be under the influence of Jesus; be strengthened, share love, and allow your world and the world around you to benefit from your influence and Enjoy!

August 29

Good Morning Sunshine! Make it a Day of Exploring! What's to explore? We're probably just going through our ordinary life doing the same ordinary things that we've already discovered; what possibly could be left to explore? Everything! Sometimes we just become so comfortable in the ordinary that we forget there is extraordinary all around us. We lose our adventurous spirit and stop exploring. You may think that you have to leave where you are and travel to new places and try new things. While this is true, and if you can do it, go for it and have fun! However, you can explore right where you are during your everyday routine. We have been created with the gift of senses, yet we limit ourselves in using them. We have eyes to see, yet we often miss or overlook how beautiful the world is. When is the last time you woke up early to see a sunrise or went on a nature walk to explore the presence of God through creation? We have the gift of hearing, but when was the last time we truly listened and found blessings in children's laughter or birds singing or actually listened to someone without our own agendas in mind? We have a sense of taste, but rather than being open to trying new foods, we stick to what we know. We have the sense of touch, but when have we really taken someone's hand into ours and really felt something and realized that blessing? Without trying to be cliché, when have you stopped smelling the flowers or recognizing someone's scent during an embrace? We have also been given a mind to think for ourselves, a mind to learn and grow in knowledge... to explore. We've been given a voice to speak up and ask questions. We are spiritual beings and able to explore the presence of God everywhere and in everything. Life is waiting... explore it and Enjoy!

August 30

Good Morning Sunshine! Make it a Day of Getting a Grip! We hold on tightly to so many things. We hang onto doubts and insecurities, fears, negative thoughts, and feelings. We hold fast to grudges and bad relationships, and difficult circumstances. We even have this death grip on the past, holding on like we can change yesterday rather than learning from it, letting go, and moving forward. We are gripping so many things, sometimes the wrong things. What if we determined that today we were going to take hold of Jesus and grip it so tightly that we would never let go? What if we made the decision to hold fast to the promises of God and the peace and love that we are offered without price or condition through Christ. What if we loosen our grip on empty promises that we can buy, or earn our happiness if we look, act, and think like the world. Psalm 91:14-16 (MSG) says: "If you'll hold on to me for dear life," says God, "I'll get you out of any trouble. I'll give you the best of care if you'll only get to know and trust me. Call me, and I'll answer, be at your side in bad times; I'll rescue you, then throw you a party. I'll give you a long life, give you a long drink of salvation!" Get a grip on God today; hold fast to love, peace, forgiveness, mercy, grace, joy, and hope! Hold onto God and your faith. If we hold onto what is true, right, and Holy, the world may never have its hold on us again. Get a Grip and Enjoy!

August 31

Good Morning Sunshine! Make it a Different Kind of Day! Well, most of us are probably following the same routine today as yesterday, so how exactly can we make it a different kind of day? You can still make today different even if you go through the same exact motions as yesterday. You can change the way you think, the way you act or react, the way you feel, and you can make it a different kind of day by being a different kind of you. If you tend to worry about everything, be different and give your concerns over to God. Can you imagine how different today would be if you focused on what you can do rather than what you can't if your focus was faith rather than fear or anxiety? If you tend to stress out because your plate is full, be different and ask for help. If you're one who tends to raise your voice, be determined to be different by responding in a calm manner with a soft voice, then wait to see the difference in those around you. You'll probably catch them off guard. If you're one to just take the day as it comes, be different and dare to seize the day. Be determined to take action and make things happen. Can you imagine how life would be if you were different in your outlook, attitude, and relationships with God and others? How different would your day be if you had expectations of today being a fabulous day and you refused to allow anyone or anything to steal your peace and joy, and you meant it? Your world would change. Who knows, you being different just may change the world around you as well! Be different and Enjoy!

September

September 1

Good Morning Sunshine! Make it a Day of Looking Up! I think sometimes we go through life visually impaired. Oh, it's not that we can't see with our eyes that's the issue; it's more a matter of the direction we choose to focus on that affects our sight. We seem to be able to look at ourselves and our own lives and often are so blinded by our own circumstances and situations that we can't see anything else. We seem to be able to look out and see obstacles and challenges very clearly before us. We can look at others and draw conclusions about their lives and make judgments. You seem our vision is impaired. In Mark 8:22-26, Jesus healed a blind man. Jesus placed his hands on the blind man's eyes. The man looked up, and his eyes were opened, his sight restored, and he could see everything clearly. When we hold our heads up high as children of God, we have no choice but to look up. When we look to Jesus and allow him to touch the eyes of our hearts, minds, and spirits, we can't help but believe and see clearly that we have a higher calling and a higher purpose. When we look up to God, we see far beyond circumstances and what is to what can be. We have a new vision and clear sight. We have hope. Have your vision checked by God today and focus on what is true and right and holy. See clearly. Look up and Enjoy!

September 2

Good Morning Sunshine! Make it a Day of Teaching Love! There is so much hatred in the world. People hate one another because of the difference in skin color, religious beliefs, economic status, sexual orientation, education, political affiliation, the country we're from... the list goes on. You name it, and we can find someone, somewhere, who hates it, or us. If you think about hatred, none of us was born hating; hatred is learned. So if we can learn to hate, then we must be able to learn to love. And if we're taught to love, and we learn to love, then we'll begin to live love. If we live to love, then others may learn love from us. We essentially become teachers of love. Seems more natural, doesn't it? We were created in love by Love itself. 1st John 4:16 tells us that God is Love. If God is Love and we were created in Love, then we too must be love. How did we forget? When did we stop learning from the right teachers? And more importantly, who and what are others learning from us? God, through Christ, has taught us the true meaning of Love. Remember you are loved; learn it, live it, share it, teach it! Teach Love and Enjoy!

September 3

Good Morning Sunshine! Make it a Day of Recognition! Andre Breton said, "To see, to hear, means nothing. To recognize or not to recognize means everything." What a powerful statement. We see injustice all around us, and we often continue on our way because it doesn't affect us, or it may be inconvenient for us to get involved. We hear of those who struggle, and we feel bad for a moment, and then we go about life as normal. We see, and we hear, but until we are convicted to do something to make a difference until we truly recognize what we see and hear, our seeing and hearing are meaningless. Matthew 13:16 Jesus is speaking to his disciples, and he says: "Blessed are your eyes because they see; and your ears because they hear." As disciples and followers of Christ, our eyes and ears have been opened, and we have recognized Jesus in our lives. We have been blessed to have our eyes see and our ears hear, and in doing so, we are now responsible for recognizing the difference we can and should make in the world for Christ's sake. What you recognize and acknowledge changes everything because knowledge obligates you to live differently. Knowledge obligates you to live justly, to love mercy, and to walk humbly with God (Micah 6:8). Recognize that YOU can and do make a difference. See where God needs you to live justly, to love mercy, and to walk humbly today. God needs you to live out the calling on your life. Hear God calling you to be the difference. Hear, See and Recognize where God needs you. YOU make a difference, and Enjoy!

September 4

Good Morning Sunshine! Make it a Day of Being Empty! The truth is we are so full of our own circumstances, feelings, and our own stuff that we don't allow room for God to get in and work in and through our lives. We are so full of us that we get in our own way, and even more than that, we get in God's way. I have heard a simple prayer that says: "God empty me of me and fill me with Thee." So when we are empty of us, God can fill us. So, get empty! Emptying ourselves allows us to take on a new way of thinking and a new way of living. Emptying ourselves enables our thoughts and attitudes to become more Christlike. If we empty ourselves of worry, we allow the Spirit of Hope to fill us. When we empty ourselves of doubt, we allow the Holy Spirit to fill us with faith to reassure us of God's promises. When we empty ourselves of self-pity, we stop looking at what we don't have or what we can't do, and we become full of the Spirit of Possibilities. Then before we know it, our dismal outlook changes from what I can get for myself to a joyful attitude of what I can do for others or even, there's nothing I can't do with God's help. When you empty you of you, then and only then is there room for the Holy Spirit of God to truly fill you. And when you are filled with the Holy Spirit, you are so full of the love of God that there's no room for anything but peace, hope, faith, joy, and love in you! Get empty, so you can become full and ENJOY!

September 5

Good Morning Sunshine! Make it a Day of Using Your Hands to Make a Difference. We use our hands for everything, and we don't give it a second thought; it just comes naturally. We don't consciously tell our hands to do anything; we think in our minds, and then our brains signal for our bodies to put those thoughts, and our hands, into action. However, what if we thought about our hands intentionally? What if we decided that everything we do with our hands today is going to make a difference? When you reach your hand out to take hold of another, whether meeting someone for the first time or holding the hand of someone you love and care about, your hands are making a difference. Your hands are extending hospitality, acceptance, and love. Be intentional. Use the power of touch that you possess in your hands. When you reach out to offer help or a hand up in life to those in need, your hands may be the difference that someone else has been searching for. Think of the ways that your hands can extend grace, compassion, generosity, and kindness to make a difference to someone else. If your hands can do all that, imagine if you put your heart, mind, and soul into everything as well. You wouldn't only use your hands to make a difference; you would use you, all of you, to make a difference. Start with your hands, and add the other parts of you as soon as possible. Make a difference and Enjoy!

September 6

Good Morning Sunshine! Make it a Day of Welcoming! Welcome today and the opportunities and possibilities that await you with open arms. Your arms, and even your hearts and minds, need to be open in order to welcome anything. Welcome new people into your life, even if it's only a 30-second conversation or a ZOOM meeting. Welcome those already in your life again. Smile, be pleasant, be kind, be loving... if you need to, use words. Welcome the chance to do something different, out of your routine. Drive a different route home, go for a walk, try new foods... welcome the chance to see and experience the world, your world, with a sense of newness and awe. Welcome opportunities to bless others with your gifts and talents or with a willing heart and spirit. Welcome living and breathing in life and its beauty. Welcome the love of God to fill you so that you may know how beautiful and precious you are, and welcome others to know this love. Open your hearts, minds, and arms today to welcome and embrace the goodness of life. Welcome others to join you and Enjoy!

September 7

Good Morning Sunshine! Make it a Day of Writing Your Own Psalm! Have you ever read the book of Psalms? The writers of the Psalms are communicating with God, sharing their deepest and most intimate feelings and emotions. They share their praises, joys, and celebrations as well as their anger, pain, loneliness, fears, and frustrations. They cry out to God in desperation, pleading for help and to have their struggles removed and circumstances changed. They sing out in praise and thanksgiving, thanking God for the blessings they've received in life, praising God for God's faithfulness. They write of their hope and their faith, and their trust in God. They sing out, thanking God for God's presence in their lives. They ask for help when they can't feel God's presence when they feel abandoned, and life seems overwhelming. The psalmists put their prayers in writing. They wrote their Psalm, their conversation, and their innermost thoughts and desires to God. The psalmists were human, just like you and me. They felt, they hurt, they rejoiced and celebrated life, and through it, all remained in conversation and connected to God. What is your Psalm today? You don't have to write it out necessarily. Yet you can share your heart, your thoughts, your hopes, your fears, and your life with God. Sing out or cry out but remain in conversation and connected to God. Write your Psalm. Share your Psalm with God, and Enjoy!

September 8

Good Morning Sunshine! Make it a Day of Living to Love! What if your purpose today were to love, nothing more and nothing less? What if you decided to love everyone, those closest to you, your family, your friends, acquaintances, or even strangers? What if you loved those who can't, or won't, love you in return? The way you express love to each person will obviously be different based on your relationships, but what if you were open to extending love and demonstrating love to everyone through your words and actions? What would happen if you were determined to love the beauty of life and creation all around you? What if you loved your job or your commute today? What if you faced your circumstances, obstacles, or challenges with a loving attitude? We have all experienced the opposite. We know of hatred, anger, violence, judgment, injustice, and intolerance... the world shows it to us all the time, and there are times we show these things to the world. But what if you lived in love today, and every day, and refused to accept anything less than living in love? The answer to the "what if's" is up to you. You have the potential to share the gift of love. The possibilities of what happens when you live love are endless. You may be the difference in someone else's life, and that may make all the difference in yours. God is love and created us to love. It seems only natural that we would live that way. Life has a way of returning to us what we give away. Live to love; live it, give it, share it, receive it and Enjoy!

September 9

Good Morning Sunshine! Make it a Day of Trying! We all want to live a full and meaningful life, go to new places, to have new experiences, or just to have circumstances be completely different than they are now. We talk about it all the time but how often do we actually try to make those changes happen? How often do we put the effort in to live a rich, full and meaningful life? We can say we want change, but we go through our same routines doing the same thing day in and day out and wonder why everything is still the same. We talk to our friends, we spend time in prayer, yet nothing changes. Change won't just happen; we have to try. God answers prayer, but we may need to put the effort in. God created us with minds to think, with voices to speak, with strength and courage beyond our own understanding, but until we actually try to use all of these gifts, nothing will ever change. Gandhi said: "You must be the change you wish to see in the world." If you want to change your world, then you need to try. If you want to change the world around you, you need to try. If you want to live life with meaning and purpose, you need to try. If you want to laugh and love, then you need to try. Try something different, try something new, try thinking new thoughts, or meeting new people. It's your life, don't let it pass you by. Try something, anything, everything, and Enjoy!

September 10

Good Morning Sunshine! Make it a Day of Being Fully Present! Do you realize that being a presence in someone's life is one of the greatest gifts you can offer? Have you ever been involved in a conversation where someone else is speaking, and in your mind, you are already thinking of a response or about anything and everything except what's actually being said while still nodding your head like you are listening? You are physically present, but your mind and heart are absent. Perhaps you have been the one speaking and realize your conversation partner is not fully present with you. Henri Nouwen said: "We have lost the simple but difficult gift of being present to each other." I can't help but think that if we are not fully present with each other, we may have also lost the gift of being fully present in life or fully present before God? I invite you to be fully present today. Be fully present with God; pray and worship with passion. Be fully present with others; look each other in the eye, pay attention and really listen, then pause and take into consideration what was said before sharing your response. Be fully present in life; take it all in, and fully give back what you can. Use the gift of your presence to make a difference. Be fully present and Enjoy!

September 11

Good Morning Sunshine! Make it a Day of Rembrance! 9/11 is a day that we will never forget. Somehow when tragedy strikes, it's indelible in our memories. We remember where we were, what we were doing, who we were with, and how we were feeling. We remember it all with explicit detail. Years later, we can recall every moment as though it happened yesterday. While we can remember the tragedy, sometimes we forget to remember hope. Today is a day that we need to remember to pray for those who lost their lives, the families they left behind & all of those who were and still are affected. We need to remember to grieve the loss of life, love, and potential. Yet we need more than ever to remember hope. Hope allows the spirit within us to be resilient, to look forward with confidence, faith, and trust in God. To truly honor those who have perished is to live our lives to their fullest, with hope, live with love, and fulfilling our potential. Our God is a God of Hope, and as a people of God, this is our gift, hope! Let hope be indelible on your hearts, in your spirits, and in your lives! Remember and Enjoy!

September 12

Good Morning Sunshine! Make it a Day of Inspiring! Did you know that you possess the gift of inspiration? Do you realize the potential you have each and every day to influence others? Most don't recognize this, and that's okay. It's not important that you make inspiring others your main objective but that you live your life in such a manner that you inspire others simply by being you. Roy T. Bennett said: "To shine your brightest light is to be who you truly are."

As a person of faith, if you live your life loving God and others, if you can see beyond what's right in front of you and choose to live in the joy of Christ despite your circumstances if you live with a positive attitude demonstrating a strong faith, hope , and trust in God's promises, if you are authentically you and live in love, you don't have to do anything different, but you will be an inspiration and inspire others so much more than you know! Go be you; live, love, inspire and Enjoy!

September 13

Good Morning Sunshine! Make it a Day of Doing All You Can! Often, we do what we have to, to get by, to not get noticed or not get involved, but we don't necessarily do all that we can. Doing all that we can involves commitment, and commitment has become an issue for many. John Wesley, the founder of Methodism, said: "Do all the good you can, by all the means you can, in all the ways you can, in all the places you can, all the times you can, to all the people you can, as long as you ever can." He also said: "Earn all you can, save all you can, give all you can." The keywords are "All You Can!" Be committed to doing all you can. Don't live doing just what you have to and half-heartedly. Do all you can, with all of your heart, for God, for others, and for yourself. If you live doing all you can, you never know who you may inspire to follow your example. Do all you can to love, to give, to share with others, and to make a difference and Enjoy!

September 14

Good Morning Sunshine! Make it a Day of Giving Back to God! I read a quote that says: "Your talent is God's gift to you. What you do with it is your gift to God." We often think of talent as having the ability to sing, dance, and create art in the form of paintings or writings and assume if we don't have these talents, then we have none. The truth is we have each been created and gifted with talents to share with the world, to make a difference, and to live out for God's purpose. Some have the talent of speaking, sharing wisdom, and offering loving, sound advice. Some are talented in seeing the needs of others and working to fill those needs. Others have the talent of being a presence in the lives of family, friends, and even strangers. We have all been gifted with talents; are you using yours? Gift God today; live out your talents and Enjoy!

September 15

Good Morning Sunshine! Make it a Day of Never Ever! Never ever doubt that God loves you and you were created with and for a purpose! Never ever underestimate yourself, your gifts and talents, or your strength and abilities. Never ever say never! Stay open to new possibilities and opportunities. Never ever tire of doing good. Never ever allow those you love to wonder how you feel about them. Never ever give up. Never ever say I can't. Never ever think that you don't make a difference because you can, and you do, make a difference. Never ever put yourself down. Never ever forget to count your blessings. Never ever take life for granted! Embrace every second and live each day to its fullest. Never ever let a day go by without loving and laughing. Never ever, even for one moment, forget how amazing you are! Never ever give up hope! Make it a day, or a lifetime, of Never Ever and Enjoy!

September 16

Good Morning Sunshine! Make it a Day of Hope and Expectation! A farmer plows and plants seeds in a field with the hope that this hard work will pay off, he has expectation of a great harvest. He is believing in his investment. We have opportunity everyday to plant seeds of a different sort, in a different field. We can invest in our lives and in the lives of others by trusting in God, learning as much as possible, loving without limits, being peacemakers, giving generously, offering compassion, etc. The list goes on. When you live with hope, you live with great expectations that the seeds planted will produce a great harvest; that your investment will pay off. Romans 12:12 says: "Rejoice in our confident hope. Be patient in trouble and keep on praying." And Galatians 6:9 says: "So let's not get tired of doing what is good. At just the right time we will reap a harvest of blessing if we don't give up." Live with hope and expectation! Believe nothing less and don't give up or stop planting! Plant seeds of faith, love, of hope and expectation, in your own heart, mind and spirit and in others. Believe there will be a great harvest and Enjoy!

September 17

Good Morning Sunshine! Make it a Day of Finding Out Why! Mark Twain said: "The two most important days in your life are the day you are born, and the day you find out why." God created you with a purpose in mind. The trick is discovering what that purpose is and then fulfilling it. Like anything in life, discovering your purpose takes effort on your part. First, you have to believe that you have a purpose and that your life can and does make a difference. Once you realize that, then you have to do the seeking, exploring, and dig a little deeper. You have to learn what you are passionate about. You have to find out why and then do all you can to live it out and incorporate your passions into your life. The other trick is to never stop finding out why because we never stop having purpose until our last earthly breath. Your purpose today may be different than your purpose tomorrow or even a year from now! Keep finding out why! Believe, explore, discover, live, share and Enjoy!

September 18

Good Morning Sunshine! Make it a Day of Being on Fire! John Wesley said: "Catch on fire, and others will love to come to watch you burn." People are automatically attracted to light, warmth, and positive energy. Did you ever notice that laughter is contagious? You may not even know why someone is laughing, but you begin to laugh as well just because you are in their presence. It's also very hard to stay in a bad mood when you are around happy, joyful people. They become contagious, and you begin to see the light, feel the warmth and gain positive energy. What if you were the one who was light? What if you carried a flame that warmed others in your presence? What if you were on fire with joy, love, peace, faith, and hope? Imagine the lives that you would touch and the sparks that you would cast onto others? Acts 13:47 says: "I have made you a light for all people so that you could bring salvation to the end of the earth." Your light, positive energy, and your bright shining flame might just catch the world on fire! The world needs light, warmth, and positive energy. Be on fire, share the flame and Enjoy!

September 19

Good Morning Sunshine! Make it a Day of Embracing Your Trials!
I have heard with trials, we grow stronger in faith. With faith, we
move closer to God, and with God, we can do all things. We always
want to escape our trials because they're not easy, they're
uncomfortable, and they can be painful. That makes sense. Yet we
know that trials will still come. Rather than trying to escape them,
what if we embraced our trials with prayer, hope, trust, and faith?
What if we believed God was with us through difficulties , and we
gathered strength in knowing we weren't alone in our struggles and
circumstances? What if we did more than that and actually put our
trials into God's hands? Then as we embrace our trials, we would
actually be embracing God. Embrace trials, have faith, move
closer to God, knowing you can do all things and Enjoy!

September 20

Good Morning Sunshine! Make it a Day of Losing It! Usually, when we lose "it," we automatically assume what we're losing is our temper or our mind. Today, choose to hang onto both your temper and your mind because losing them will cause you to lose your peace. Never let anything get you to the point where you lose your peace. Instead, lose other things. Lose negative thoughts and attitudes. Lose looking for validation and affirmation from others and be confident in who God created you to be. If those things come, embrace them and give thanks but don't wait for them to define you or encourage you. Lose your fears and anxieties and cling to your faith. Lose only seeing with your eyes and begin seeing with your heart. It will help you to see how much more beautiful the world is. Lose burdens and walk a little lighter. Lose it, all of it, and Enjoy!

September 21

Good Morning Sunshine! Make it a Day of Being Defined by Love! Daphne Rose Kingma wrote in a passage called "Real Love," – "For it is in loving, as well as in being loved, that we become most truly ourselves. No matter what we do, say, accomplish, or become, it is our capacity to love that ultimately defines us. In the end, nothing we do or say in this lifetime will matter as much as the way we have loved one another." The Scriptures tell us to love one another repeatedly: 1 Peter 4:8: "Above all, love each other deeply because love covers over a multitude of sins." John 15:12: "My command is this: Love each other as I have loved you." We live in a world where it has become easier to hate than to love. It has become easier to judge than to accept. It has become easier to ignore someone than to reach out to help someone. It has become easier to live in silence than to speak up for justice. Let us not be defined by our capacity to hate, judge, or ignore. Let us be defined by our capacity to love. We were created by God in love, to be love, share love, and to love God and to love one another. Let your capacity to love define you today and always and Enjoy!

September 22

Good Morning Sunshine! Make it a Day of Best Things! Someone recently shared a quote with me: "Good things come to those who Believe. Better things come to those who are Patient, and the Best Things come to those who Don't Give Up." We all want the "Best Things" but often stop striving for them when life and circumstances seem too difficult or overwhelming. We give up and wave our white flags in surrender. Everyone has challenges, but it's those who don't give up in the face of adversity who receive the "Best Things" in life. What are some of those best things? Strong character, a sense of self-worth and value, achievement of dreams and goals, faith, hope and trust in God, purpose, and meaning... and I'm just getting started. Galatians 6:9 says: "Let us not become weary in doing good, for at the proper time we will reap a harvest if we do not give up." God wants us to keep striving, to keep giving it our all to achieve our goals, and to keep trying to obtain the best things in life. Don't give up, ever... the Best Things are waiting. Keep going and Enjoy!

September 23

Good Morning Sunshine! Make it a Day of Astounding Yourself! Thomas Edison said: "If we all did the things we are capable of, we would astound ourselves!" This is how we should live, believing that we can do anything and that our potential is limitless, from the smallest of tasks to the largest of achievements. If you want to accomplish goals or make your dreams come true, you must believe that you are capable. Once you know you are, do all you can to make things happen! First, pray. You can do all things through Christ who strengthens you. Dream, believe, work hard, ask for help along the way and pray again. Before you know it, you'll be astounded when you realize that you were capable after all. Astound yourself today by living out your full potential, and Enjoy!

September 24

Good Morning Sunshine! Make it a Day of Hello and Goodbye! It's not easy saying hello or goodbye because both mean some sort of change, and no one likes change. Yet, both hello and goodbye are necessary every day. Today we need to say hello to a new day, a fresh start, a chance to right wrongs, and the endless possibilities ahead of us. We also need to say goodbye to yesterday, along with the past, any mistakes that we've made, and things we cannot change. We should say hello to opportunities of meeting new people and establishing new relationships, learning new things, and going on new adventures. We should say hello to forgiving ourselves and others by saying goodbye to pains and hurts that we've inflicted or received. You can't fully say hello to the newness of life that each day offers without having a goodbye to the past. Learn from yesterday, but tell it goodbye, then look forward to today and embrace it with a hello and Enjoy!

September 25

Good Morning Sunshine! Make it a Day of Making It! If you choose to make it a fantastic day, it will be. If you choose to make it a beautiful day, it will be! If you choose to make it a day where you see goodness in the world, you will see it. If you choose to make it a day of getting things done, you'll work hard, and it will happen. If you choose to make it a day of love and laughter, you will love and be loved, and you will laugh. The best part of all of this is you get to make it whatever kind of day, or life, you choose. But you need to make choices, intentional, not always easy, choices. By the way, your choices affect not only you but also everyone around you; choose wisely! Your choices to see beauty, to love and laugh, to have a fantastic day may help others make those same choices for themselves. Make it awesome, and Enjoy!

September 26

Good Morning Sunshine! Make it a Day of Abundance! Did you ever wonder what happened to the abundance of dreams, hope, faith, and love you had as a child? Time has taught us to lose heart and courage, to stop believing, and give up on dreams. The world has shouted to live this way or that. However, God whispers and tells us to be abundantly courageous! Have abundant confidence to dream big and to believe. Having a heart filled with abundant unconditional love and abundant peace is possible in all circumstances. Hang onto the abundance of peace that is yours through faith. You'll have to listen closely to God's whisper in the midst of the world's shouting. Yet when you focus on God, you can receive the true, abundant gifts that God has for you. Listen carefully to the abundant whispers of love and encouragement from God and once again, as children of God, reclaim your abundance of dreams, peace, hope, faith , and love and Enjoy!

September 27

Good Morning Sunshine! Make it a Day of Becoming a Gift! I read that we become the gift we give. With that in mind, wouldn't it be great if we gave away the gift of love; real, true, unconditional love, not looking for anything in return. If we gave love away, that is exactly what we would become. Give away the gifts of joy and laughter, forgiveness and acceptance, compassion and mercy, and become all of these things. You see, the gift we give is ourselves. Give away the gift of you and the love of Jesus in you, and become more Christ-like. The world is getting what we are giving out, and we are becoming what we give; give away the good stuff that's a rare and true gift these days. Give it away! Give you away and become a gift and Enjoy!

September 28

Good Morning Sunshine! Make it a Day of Standing Back Up! Every once in a while, life has a way of knocking you down, or circumstances seem to get you down, and then your own thoughts often keep you down. It's not a matter of if but when stuff happens. We will feel like the carpet was pulled beneath us. The issue is not what knocks us down, gets us down, or tries to keep us down. The issue is whether or not we choose to stand back up. 1 Peter 5 speaks of standing firm in faith in spite of suffering (getting knocked down) and how faith in Christ will restore, support, and strengthen us and provide a firm foundation to stand. "Stand firm in this grace." The key word here... Stand! You are a child of the Most High God; stand up in the face of adversity. Stand strong in the midst of challenges. Stand back up if you get knocked down. If God is for you, who or what can come against you! Stand tall, stand strong, stand with others, and when you're standing, help others stand too! Stand and Enjoy!

September 29

Good Morning Sunshine! Make it a Day of Taking It to God. We see horrific things taking place in the world; we take it in. We see the pain and suffering of others; we take it in. When we struggle in our own lives, we carry it within. When we become angry or frustrated, we vent it, often in the wrong direction. When we have joy and celebrations, we hang onto it and treasure it. When we're afraid and anxious, we allow it to hinder our lives. You see, we have all of these "its"; sadness, pain, suffering and struggles, anger and frustration, fears and anxieties, joys and celebrations and we keep them, carry them, take them out on others, and we take them in and hang onto them when God is saying bring it, whatever "it" is to me. I will help you, be with you, encourage you, support you, and love you through it, but you need to bring it to me. 1 Peter 5:7 says: "Give all your worries and cares to God, for he cares about you." So take your worries, anxieties, cares, burdens, anger, and frustrations, even your joys and excitement, to God. Take your life to God, all of it, and Enjoy!

September 30

Good Morning Sunshine! Make it a Day of Breaking Out! Have you ever felt that you were held captive by your circumstances, choices, or thoughts? Everyone has, but the truth is we have the capability to break out, to be free. We can challenge our thoughts, change our routines and make different decisions. We can choose to break out of bad habits, negative thinking, and poor choices. Yet, often we get stuck and somehow become comfortable in our discomfort. We fear change, even if it's for the better. Break out! Yes, it's easier said than done, but not impossible! Scripture tells us that we can do all things through Christ who strengthens us. Look to Jesus for strength and guidance and if you don't like your circumstances, change them. If you can't change them, then pray and change your heart and attitude, and your way of thinking. If you find yourself thinking negatively, challenge and redirect your thoughts. Many times, you are the only one holding yourself captive. Breakout, be free, and Enjoy!

October

October 1

Good Morning Sunshine! Make it a Day of Anything Can Be! I read a great quote by Shel Silverstein that said: "Listen to the mustn'ts child, listen to the don'ts. Listen to the shouldn'ts, the impossibles, the wonts. Listen to the never haves, then listen close to me... anything can happen child, anything can be." You want happiness? Don't wait for it. Choose to be happy, believe it , and never let go of if. You want peace? Choose peace! Strive for it and obtain it, and don't let it out of your grasp. You want love? Then love without limits and conditions and you will receive love beyond measure! You want to move forward? Then quit being stuck in the past. You see, anything can be! Impossibilities come from our own doubts and fears or from listening to others. Stop believing in impossibilities and embrace possibilities that Anything Can Be and Enjoy!

October 2

Good Morning Sunshine! Make it a Day of Being Empowered! Sir Francis Bacon said: "Knowledge is power." Gaining knowledge is a combination of a desire to learn, a willingness to grow, and enough humility to use your knowledge to make a difference to others. Having a great wealth of knowledge empowers because it creates confidence. The power behind knowledge is the fact that knowledge obligates you. Once you know something, you can't un-know it, so you must choose to use the power of your knowledge to make a difference or to ignore what you know. It's your choice, and this empowers you. What do you choose to do with your knowledge today? I would encourage you to learn as much as possible through experiences, through reading, through the wisdom of others, and for those of faith, through the Scriptures and the example of Jesus Christ. Once you have knowledge of Jesus, you cannot "un-know" it, so you either need to choose to live out that knowledge in all you say and do or ignore it. Every person, every encounter, and every experience will teach you something; choose to learn and gain knowledge. Proverbs 18:15 says: "Intelligent people are always ready to learn. Their ears are open for knowledge." Be confident in who you are and take your knowledge, and make a difference in the world. Be empowered and Enjoy!

October 3

Good Morning Sunshine! Make it a Day of Being the Embrace of God! An Embrace is "to clasp tightly in the arms, especially with affection, to cherish, to cling together." Our God is a God of love and compassion, mercy and grace. We were created in God's image and have been called the hands and feet of Jesus Christ. We're told that the Holy Spirit lives in and through us. If this is the case and you believe it to be true, then you are love and compassion. You are mercy and grace. And if you are all of these things, then when you reach out and take someone into your arms, you become the embrace of God for another. Every time you open your heart in love or your mind in understanding to someone, you become the embrace of God. So go and embrace others, some in body, some in mind, all in spirit. Clasp tightly, especially with affection , and to cherish and cling together. Be the Embrace of God and Enjoy!

October 4

Good Morning Sunshine! Make it a Day to Be an Inspiration to Others. You know, inspiration or to inspire is to breathe life into... so what I'm suggesting is no easy task. In order to inspire, affect, influence, or to spark something in someone else, in order to breathe life into others, you must be inspired and full of life yourself; how can you give away what you don't have? This is not necessarily something you can do in words, but in heart and in the life, you lead. Are you inspiring others? Did you ever take a step back to see what your contribution is to the world? Is your life inspiring the people around you? Are you breathing life into those who need it? Don't think this is something huge or unattainable. Have you made someone smile or shared a smile of your own? Do you have a positive attitude when your circumstances indicate you shouldn't? Do you live a life of faith, and do you have hope? Do you laugh and enjoy life? Have you spoken a kind word or helped someone in need? Have you shared the love of Christ by extending grace and love? See, you are an inspiration! Keep up the good work, and Enjoy!!

October 5

Good Morning Sunshine! Make it a Day of Walking! Steve Maraboli said: "Happiness, success, excellence: they are not something you get for knowing the path; they are something you experience by walking it." We live and experience life by participation. We can't just sit on the sidelines and hope that life, happiness, success, and excellence will just magically come to us. While they may come near us, they will certainly pass us by if we, if YOU, don't begin walking to greet and embrace them. Leave the watching behind and begin walking. Put on your walking shoes of faith and hope, and walk with determination and courage. Know the path you want to follow and start walking it! Walk in the power and presence of God, embrace the journey and find your life's happiness, success, and excellence, and Enjoy!

October 6

Good Morning Sunshine! Make it a Day of Staying the Course! You could also call this hold on, be determined, or keep going. All of these mean to persevere in the face of adversity or difficulty. Our first inclination is to give up, turn around or let go when life gets hard. We often find ourselves in a place of self-pity and asking why me. It's at this very moment you must make a crucial choice, to stay the course or to give up. But in order to get to where you want to be, you have got to go through what is. Romans 12:12 says: "Rejoice in our confident hope. Be patient in trouble and keep on praying," and Galatians 6:9: "Let's not tire of doing good. At just the right time, we'll reap a harvest of blessing if we don't give up." Never give up; stay the course and Enjoy!

October 7

Good Morning Sunshine! Make it a Day of Loving Life! Love every part of life, the good, the not-so-good, and everything in between. There is a lot of good in life to love, people, the Sun, Moon, and stars, laughter, hugs, flowers, food, hard work, learning, and growing, and I'm just getting started! Believe it or not, there is a lot to love in the not-so-good. Challenges are uncomfortable, and obstacles can be frustrating, yet it is in adversity that our true character is defined. You may not love your circumstances, but you can love who you are and how you handle them. You can love the in-between where life may seem dull and mundane. I read a quote that says: "One day your life will flash before your eyes. Make sure it's worth watching." You don't get today twice! Make sure it's worth watching! Love life and Enjoy!

October 8

Good Morning Sunshine! Make it a Day of Nourishing Your Mind! The best way to nourish your mind is to begin with positive thoughts. They say attitude is everything. If you have positive thoughts, you can't help but have a positive attitude. When you share yourself with the world, what is it you would like the world to see in you and remember? Your thoughts and attitude affect everyone around you as well. Nourish your mind and think positive! Be grateful for your blessings and for others in your life. Giving thanks for the goodness around you has a way of nourishing your body, mind, and spirit. Surround yourself with positive people. Read and learn as much as possible. Exercise, take a walk, and breathe in nature. Pray, meditate, and be still in God's presence. Proverbs 4:23 says: "Be careful how you think; your life is shaped by your thoughts." Nourish your mind well, and you'll shape your life well. Your well-nourished mind can make a difference in your life and the lives of others. Feed it well, and Enjoy!

October 9

Good Morning Sunshine! Make it a Day of Being Blessed to Be a Blessing! Jack Hyles said: "The greatest blessing in the world is being a blessing." Did you ever realize that you have the potential to change lives or bless others? Well, you do! A simple smile or kind gesture can make all the difference in the world. Being a listening ear, a shoulder to cry on, a voice of reason, the one who will join in to help when a friend is in a bind, or one who will pray for another, can change someone's entire perspective, attitude, or outlook on life. Just being present without a word can speak volumes. Being lighthearted and joyful can lift the spirits of those around you. Scripture tells us that laughter is the best medicine! Your generosity in donating time, gifts, talents, resources, and money to church or charities blesses many more than you will ever realize. Live up to your blessing potential! God didn't add another day to your life because you needed it. God did it because someone out there needs you! Bless others, be blessed, and a blessing, and Enjoy!

October 10

Good Morning Sunshine! Make it a Day of Enjoying Your Daily Bread! When we pray the Lord's Prayer and say, "Give us this day our daily bread," we're asking God to sustain us this day. Yet we have this habit of looking back and reaching out for yesterday's day-old bread or looking too far ahead at the bread that hasn't even been baked yet. Sort of like eating breakfast while planning dinner. Who hasn't done that? This bread I'm referring to is our past, present, and future. While we can look to our past and see how God sustained us through it and we can learn from it, we can't stay there. That bread is stale. We can look ahead to set goals and put a plan in place to achieve them, but we can't forget where we are to get where we're going. That bread needs time to rise. Ask God to give you what you need to sustain you today and give you your daily bread. Taste the goodness of today and Enjoy!

October 11

Good Morning Sunshine! Make it a Day of Deciding to be the Person You Want to Be! The world will tell you who they think you are, and many times you'll believe it. People will tell you what direction to take throughout the course of your life, and many times, you'll follow, even against your own better judgment. Either way, others will determine who you are if you don't know who you are and if you let them. However, Ralph Waldo Emerson said: "The only person you are destined to become is the person you decide to be." Take heed to the words "you decide" because you have been created with your own voice to speak up and your own mind to think for yourself! Yes, circumstances will often dictate paths along your journey, but along the way, you still have to decide who you want to be and how you travel. Decide who YOU want to be and then become the best you possible and Enjoy!

October 12

Good Morning Sunshine! Make it a Day of Living Happiness! We live with many things, yet happiness and joy either allude us or only allow us momentary glimpses. We seem to allow fear, disappointment, frustration, or discouragement to dwell in us and around us much longer. Happiness can be lived every moment of every day if you choose to live it. It's your choice. Denis Waitley says: "Happiness cannot be traveled to, owned, earned, or worn. It is the spiritual experience of living every minute with love, grace, and gratitude." So love as much as possible. Extend grace to everyone, choose to see your blessings rather than your burdens, and be thankful. Live with love, grace, and gratitude , and you'll be Living Happiness before you know it! Enjoy!

October 13

Good Morning Sunshine! Make it a Day of Before! I recently read the six ethics of life, and they all begin with the word "Before." Before you pray, believe. Before you speak, listen. Before you spend, earn. Before you react, think. Before you quit, try, and before you die, live. We tend to be "after" people. We believe it when we see it, not before we pray for whatever "it" is. We speak more often than we listen. We spend far more than we earn. We react on instinct or emotion rather than thinking things through and reacting rationally. We give up before trying because the tasks before us seem too difficult. And many of us are just existing and trying to get through life rather than living life. Are you a "before" person or an "after" person? It's never too late to be a Before person. So today, before you do anything, believe, listen, earn, think, try, live and Enjoy!

October 14

Good Morning Sunshine! Make it a Day of Toning It Up! Has anyone ever told you to tone it down, curb your enthusiasm, chill out, simmer down or get a grip? Come on; you've been told at least one of these. Well, today, I'm going to encourage you to tone it up and share your faith and your joy! Release your enthusiasm that it might be contagious! Don't chill out but warm up by allowing God's light and love to shine in you, and through you, onto others around you. Matthew 5:14-15 says: "You are the light of the world—like a city on a hilltop that cannot be hidden. No one lights a lamp and then puts it under a basket. Instead, a lamp is placed on a stand, where it gives light to everyone in the house." And don't simmer down; let the fire or passion in your heart be used to make a difference. Don't scare anyone in the process but live your faith out loud and lead others by example. Live in joy and happiness! Live in light and love! Tone it up and Enjoy!

October 15

Good Morning Sunshine! Make it a Day of As Much As You Can! Did you ever think how life would be if we were all determined to do, be, give, pray, love, give thanks to God, stand up for those in need, listen, learn, hope, smile, never give up and laugh as much as you can? So many of us are recipients of others around us doing as little as possible to get by, and it's frustrating. I'm sure many of us have also been dispensers of as little as possible to others at times and caused frustration. John Wesley is attributed as saying: "Do all the good you can, By all the means you can, In all the ways you can, In all the places you can. At all the times you can, To all the people you can, As long as ever you can." He's saying to live life the best you can and to help others in any way that you can. Life is far too short to live in a state of as little as possible or do what you can to get by. If you want to fully embrace life and the blessings in it, then you must live with an attitude and spirit of "As Much As You Can." Be determined to live life as much as you can today and every day, and Enjoy!

October 16

Good Morning Sunshine! Make it a Day of Doubting Your Fears! Why is it so easy for us to doubt our hopes and dreams but allow our fears to exist without question? We find it easy to compare ourselves to others and then doubt our own abilities. We doubt success, so we don't take chances. We doubt possibilities and opportunities and never try anything new. We stay where we are and feel stuck in our circumstances, and don't take chances because we doubt who we are and who we can become. We doubt that better days are coming. Why is it easier for us to believe in our fears that hinder our lives rather than believe in hope and have faith in God that can propel our lives forward? What if we determined to doubt our fears and question their existence and instead believe that we could accomplish anything before us, believing that with God, all things are possible? Doubt your fears and impossibilities and believe God has created you with a purpose, then live it. Doubt your fears, and Enjoy!

October 17

Good Morning Sunshine! Make it a Day of Not Saying I Can't! Did you ever count how many times in a day that you say, "I can't?" We say it much more than we realize. You can say "I can't" all you want, but the truth is, you can but choose not to. Saying "I can't" limits us and hinders our ability to see and realize what might be possible if we said "I'll give it a try" or "maybe I can." I can't become a great excuse for I won't. Every impossibility begins with I can't. Never restrict yourself by your own thoughts and words. Remove the limitations of "I can't," and you might just be amazed at what you can do, accomplish, achieve or become! Scripture says we CAN do all things through Christ who strengthens us! Every possibility begins with I can! Choose I can, believe I can, and Enjoy!

October 18

Good Morning Sunshine! Make it a Day of Creating What's Meant to Be! From the time we're children, we begin to form thoughts and ideas of how life is supposed to be. We have perfect images in our minds of homes, cars, and possessions that will complete our picture. We see a perfect partner by our side, holding our hand as we walk off into the sunset. We'll have the perfect job and perfect friends and a life with lots of fun and no worries and no struggles. This would all be great, but the images and ideas aren't realistic, and yet somehow, we've come to believe that our lives are less than they should be because the picture in our minds doesn't match our reality. Here's the good news. You are the artist of your own life. You get to create, develop or change the picture. In fact, every day, you have a brand-new pallet and can start over. Stop living what you think is supposed to be and start creating what is meant to be. Create your own picture, your own life, then live it perfectly and Enjoy

October 19

Good Morning Sunshine! Make it a Day of Tipping the Scales! It has been said that for every minute spent angry, we lose 60 seconds of happiness. The same could be said for all the negativity we harbor; sadness, frustration, disappointment, unforgiveness, and hatred. We are human, and we are going to feel these emotions from time to time, so to say to anyone that you should not feel negative emotions wouldn't be realistic. But there is a huge difference between experiencing negative emotions and harboring them. It is also true that you can't get the time you have spent feeling down or having negative thoughts and emotions back. The key here is to tip the scales by dedicating more of our lives to living with a positive attitude, not allowing anyone or anything to steal our peace, finding joy and harbor blessings, and allowing goodness and positivity to far outweigh the negative. We need to tip the scales in favor of happiness. Not always easy, but not impossible! Tip the scales, be happy, and Enjoy!

October 20

Good Morning Sunshine! Make it a Day of Making a Difference! Jarrod Kintz said: "Whether you live to be 50 or 100 makes no difference if you've made no difference in the world." We have tremendous potential to change the world, to leave our mark , and to make a difference. It may not be written in books or on the news, but your life is meant to make a difference in the world and to the people in it. Feeding the hungry, standing up for social justice, praying, loving, giving your time, being generous with your resources, volunteering, demonstrating faith, laughing and staying positive in difficult moments, and hugging; these are all ways that you can make a difference. Believe it or not, making a difference to others will make all the difference to you. I dare you to try it and find out! Make a difference in the world, or at least in the small portion of the world around you and Enjoy!

October 21

Good Morning Sunshine! Make it a Day of Being Sunlight! Jess Lair said, "Praise is like sunlight to the human spirit. We cannot flower and grow without it!" So if you offer praise and use your words to encourage, support, build up and empower, then you are sunlight and have amazing potential to help another human spirit grow. Every smile, every kind word, and gesture, and every interaction with someone can alter or influence their day. When you live shining light, you are letting others know that they are loved, cared for, and noticed; you are letting others know that they matter. Shining light to others doesn't diminish your own light but strengthens you to shine brighter. Give compliments, smile, and make your laughter and joy contagious. Listen and reach out to share your light. Your life is meant to shine the light that the human spirit can flower and grow! Be Sunlight and Enjoy!

October 22

Good Morning Sunshine! Make it a Day of Having Courage! Maya Angelou said: "Courage is the most important of all the virtues because, without courage, you can't practice any other virtue consistently." It takes courage to live a life of joy in the face of adversity. It takes courage to get back up if you feel as though you've been knocked down. It takes courage to face obstacles and challenges and move forward anyway. It takes courage to love or to love again if your heart's been broken. It takes courage to trust when you've been hurt, disappointed, and let down. It takes courage to have faith and to live out your convictions when the world is pulling you in a different way. It takes courage to stand up for social justice for all and to be a voice that speaks for those who are marginalized. It takes courage to be happy and to follow your dreams. But to fully live and to fully engage in the life you must have the courage to do all of these things and more. Scripture tells us in Joshua 1:9: "Be strong and courageous. Do not be afraid or discouraged. For the Lord, your God, will be with you wherever you go." Knowing that God is with you everywhere you go should give you courage. So, be courageous enough to live fully and Enjoy!

October 23

Good Morning Sunshine! Make it a Dy of Realizing Life is Too Short! We hear others say it, and we may even say it ourselves. We look back at years gone by and become conscious of how quickly time passes but do we really live as though life is too short? If we did remind ourselves daily, perhaps we would do things differently. We might be determined to make this day awesome by enjoying every moment. We might laugh more and stress less. We might live without fear of what others think of us and how we look and act. We might be more compassionate and more generous to those in need. We might take chances and not be afraid to make mistakes. We might take time to breathe in the beauty of the world around us. We might live out our faith in God, believing all things are possible. We might love passionately, hugging longer, saying I love you as much as possible to those we care about, and really loving our neighbors as we love ourselves. My friends, there is no time for "might." Life is far too short, so live today and every day to its fullest and Enjoy!

October 24

Good Morning Sunshine! Make it a Day Worth Remembering! So many of our days go by, and we don't remember what happened. Much of our time simply begins to blend together, nothing special, the same old same old. Every day we're given is a gift and a blessing. Every day of life is special, yet we treat it as ordinary. Make today different. Do something to make today worth remembering. Express love, share your faith and enthusiasm, explore your dreams, set goals , and take a step to make them happen. Sing, dance, laugh, help someone in need, do something nice for yourself but do something to remind you that today was worth it! Seize opportunities to do, to be, to become, to overcome, to embrace blessings, to love, to give, to forgive, to make every moment count, because it does! This day will never happen again; make it worth remembering and Enjoy!

October 25

Good Morning Sunshine! Make it a Day of Making Promises To YOU! Have you ever promised yourself anything? Did you ever care so much for your own well-being that you promised to take care of your body, mind, and spirit? If you have, great! If you haven't, there's no time like the present! Promise you that you will only think good thoughts about yourself. Once you believe in your own goodness and beauty, then you will be able to see goodness and beauty in others. Promise to love you for who you are, yet be open to the person God is still having you become! You then may be able to look at others in love as they are on their journey to "becoming" as well. Make a promise to seek God's peace and once you have it, promise to never allow anyone or anything to take it from you again. Promise you to have a positive attitude, to laugh as much as possible, and to not take yourself so seriously. Promise you to cling to God's promises and live in faith, hope, and trust. Your promises to you can change the world around you, or at least the way you see it! Promise You and Enjoy!

October 26

Good Morning Sunshine! Make it a Day of Gathering Strength! Life can be exhausting. Circumstances can wear us out. But it is precisely at these moments that we need to seek those things that will help us gather our strength. Begin with prayer. We have heard it said that we stand the tallest and the strongest when on our knees. Pray and know that through Christ who strengthens you, you can do all things. Read scripture. Isaiah 41:10 says: "Don't be afraid for I am with you. Don't be discouraged, for I am your God. I will strengthen you and help you. I will hold you up with my victorious right hand." Get some rest! Seems like a simple solution, yet we often ignore the fact that our body, mind, and spirit could use some downtime. Ask for help if you need it. Spend time with those who have positive energy and who will support you and encourage you. Knowing God is with us, and we are not alone, getting some rest, surrounding ourselves with friends and family who love us, clinging to scriptures, and praying will give us strength. Gather it, share it, live it and Enjoy!

October 27

Good Morning Sunshine! Make it a Day of being Liberated from Fear! I read a powerful quote by Marianne Williamson that says it all: "Our deepest fear is not that we are inadequate. Our deepest fear is that we are powerful beyond measure. We ask ourselves, "Who am I to be brilliant, gorgeous, talented, fabulous?" Actually, who are you not to be? You are a child of God. Your playing small does not serve the world. There is nothing enlightened about shrinking so that other people won't feel insecure around you. We are all meant to shine, as children do. We were born to make manifest the glory of God that is within us. It's not just in some of us; it's in everyone. And as we let our own light shine, we unconsciously give other people permission to do the same. As we are liberated from our own fear, our presence automatically liberates others." You are a child of God! Never ever forget that! Shine your light! Be liberated from fear! Liberate others and Enjoy!

October 28

Good Morning Sunshine! Make it a Day of Living For God! In Scripture, Colossians 3:23 tells us that we should work as though we are working for God and not for people. If you have a difficult job, a challenging boss or task that you just don't want to do, changing your perspective can change everything. Work as though your only goal is to glorify God. While you are at it, what if you used the same viewpoint and attitude in every aspect of life. What if you loved others as though glorifying God depended upon it? What if you help others and care for others and were generous with your resources as though your relationship with God and glorifying God depended upon them. Well, it should be no great surprise that your work, the way you love, the way you help others, your generosity and your life all depend upon how you allow the glory of God to be shown to the world through you. Your relationship with God matters that much! Live for God! Give God the glory and Enjoy!

October 29

Good Morning Sunshine! Make it a Day of Dreaming, Hoping, Believing! When you have dreams, hopes, and aspirations, what you're really saying to yourself is that you can see beyond what is and put your hope in what can be. You believe in possibilities. To the world, your dreams may not seem rational, and there may be no reason behind them, yet you still believe. It's the same as having faith in God. To much of the world, it seems as though it's not rational, and there's no reason behind it, yet you still believe. Hebrews 11:1 says, "Faith is the confidence that what we hope for will actually happen. It gives us assurance about things we cannot see." The world would be very different from the way we know it if those who had gone before us hadn't had hopes and dreams. Imagine the impact you have on those who follow you if you strive to make your dreams and aspirations come to fruition. Have faith, see beyond what is, to what can be. Dream, hope, believe, and Enjoy!

October 30

Good Morning Sunshine! Make it a Day of Slowing Down Time! Okay, we know this is impossible. Time is something that we can't stop or slow down no matter how much we want to. We look back and see how quickly time has gone by; years have flown, children have grown, and we still feel young inside, but the mirror tells a slightly different story. We live rushed lives with busy schedules, and time escapes us. Although slowing time isn't an option, we have the choice to make every moment count. The moment we're in right now will never happen again. Are you breathing it in? Are you living this moment in joy, in hope, in love? Do you cherish the time spent with family and friends? Do you tell those you love how you feel about them as often as possible? Do you take time for yourself and time to enjoy life? Time may be fleeting, but moments can last a lifetime! Slow down, breathe them in and Enjoy!

October 31

Good Morning Sunshine! Make it a Day of Calling It Quits! Doesn't sound like much of a word of inspiration, does it? I guess that all depends on what you're quitting. Try quitting the belief that you're not special or good enough. You have been fearfully and wonderfully made, created from love to be, share and receive love. You have been designed specifically with meaning and purpose. Quit comparing your gifts and talents with others and find yours! While you have breath, you have a purpose. Call it quits in believing that you're alone and start to live out the promises of God. You may be on your own in many things and various ways, but never alone; God is with you and promises to always be with you. Call it quits in negative thinking. Look for the positive, the bright side, the silver lining in every situation! If you look for it, you will find it! Call it quits from engaging in anything that hinders you from living fully in faith, hope, and love. Call it quits and Enjoy!

November

November 1

Good Morning Sunshine! Make it a Day of Using Your Power of Choice! We only have one life to live. This is your life, and you have the power to choose how to live it. You may not always be able to choose your circumstances, but you can choose your thoughts, your attitude, or your outlook in every situation. No one can choose them for you, no matter how much you'd like to blame others. People can enhance your happiness and joy, but no one is responsible for your happiness and joy but you! Choose to be happy! Happiness is a choice. Choose to find joy. Joy is a choice. Choose to challenge your thoughts of I can't to I can. You have the power to choose love, to love God, to love others, to love yourself. Use your power of choice to make your life happy. Whether you know it or not, your choices are on display for the world to see. Are you showing joy, happiness, love, or something else? Who knows, your choices just may influence others to choose more wisely for themselves. Use your power of choice to make wise choices. Choose to live in joy and love. Choose to have a positive attitude. Choose to be happy! Use your power of choice wisely, and Enjoy!

November 2

Good Morning Sunshine! Make it a 'Thanksgiving' Day! Oh, I realize that the holiday of Thanksgiving, "turkey day," is still a couple of weeks away, but did you ever think about all you have and take the time to give proper thanks for it? Now I don't just mean giving thanks for your tangible stuff, but yes, you can, and should, give thanks for all of that, too. When making today Veteran's Day, a Thanks Giving Day, I'm actually referring to all you can't reach out and grasp hold of with your hands, things like your freedoms, safety, choices, rights, and liberties. Did you ever give thanks for those? We can say what we'd like, make our own choices on lifestyle, choose our field of profession, live where we want, love whom we want, travel freely, come and go as we please, and hold a peaceful protest if we want to, receive an education, vote and worship our God freely without persecution. Did you ever think about or stop to give thanks for these types of things? There are many who serve, or have served, in our military and sacrifice time, family and life to ensure that we, people they don't even know, can have and do and live with freedoms. Do all you can today to thank those who have provided you with these privileges. See someone in uniform, say "thank you." Know a veteran? Call, visit, and reach out to let them know your appreciation. Pray and give thanks to God, who, by Grace, gives us all free will to make our own life choices. Happy Thanks Giving! Enjoy!

November 3

Good Morning Sunshine! Make it a Day of Holding On! I don't think you would be shocked if I told you that life can be hard, circumstances can be overwhelming, and obstacles can appear insurmountable. Unfortunately, we are not surprised because we have had experience. When we encounter struggle, pain, suffering, or hardship, we may feel like giving up, giving in, or letting go, but these are precisely the moments we need to remind ourselves to hold on. Hold onto the promises of God; you are loved and never alone. Hold onto family and friends and those who truly care for you. Hold onto the things you love and the things that make up who you are. Hold onto your faith , and always, always, always hold onto hope! Hold on and Enjoy!

November 4

Good Morning Sunshine! Make it a Day of Leaving Footprints! We each have the opportunity to leave our footprints, to make an impression, to set an example, to live a life that others may follow. The way you live your life can prompt others to want to follow the footprints you've left behind or turn in the other direction. You have amazing potential to leave footprints that leads to unconditional love, acceptance, and kindness. If you're generous with your gifts, talents, and resources, someone just may follow your lead. If you extend forgiveness and offer grace, you may guide others to do the same. If you choose to live in joy in spite of your circumstances, you may be living out the example that someone else needs to follow. Your life and your actions make an impression on the world. Leave footprints that make a positive difference and an impression that others will want to follow and Enjoy!

November 5

Good Morning Sunshine! Make it a Day of Looking for God! Criss Jami said: "A common mistake we make is that we look for God in places where we ourselves wish to find God, yet even in the physical reality, this is a complete failure. For example, if you lost your car keys, you would not search where you want to search; you would search where you must, in order to find them." In Jeremiah 29:13, God says: "You will seek me and find me when you seek me with all your heart." Perhaps the best place to begin looking for God is from within, your heart, your mind, your spirit, and your vision. Once you find God within and realize that God created you and is living in and through you, you can't help but see God and find God everywhere. Don't just look for God where you want to. Look for God where you must and Enjoy!

November 6

Good Morning Sunshine! Make it a Day of Being in God's Word. I know, who has time for that? The truth is, we have time, or make time, for those things that are important to us. God's Word should be important to us for so many reasons. God's Word has incredible power to motivate, guide, and sustain us, yet we often neglect to read the scriptures or spend time in study. God's Word can lift our spirits, provide strength, offer hope, and if you read it with an open heart and listening ear, God's Word can speak to you. I can't guarantee you'll hear an audible voice, but you will have the opportunity to hear God's voice in your heart if you're open to hearing it. God actually speaks to us every day through nature around us, through little blessings, through other people, but especially through the Scriptures. Can you hear it? Give it a try. You have nothing to lose but everything to gain. At the very least, it might make your day or make your day just a little bit better! Be in God's Word and Enjoy!

November 7

Good Morning Sunshine! Make it a Day of Taking Notice! Did you ever take notice, really take notice, of life around you? If you've spent any time people-watching, you should be in awe that we're all created so uniquely. While there may be similarities, there are no two alike. Did you ever take the time to take in the beauty of the changing seasons? They seem to happen right before our eyes, but do we take notice? Have you ever been in awe of a sunrise or sunset because you stopped everything from taking notice of them? Have you ever heard a child's laughter, whether you know them or not, and you smiled or laughed along with them because you took notice of simple joys that make a child happy, and it made you happy too. Betty Smith said: "Look at everything as though you were seeing it either for the first or the last time. Then your time on earth will be filled with glory." Take notice of life today, be filled with glory. Repeat again tomorrow, and Enjoy!

November 8

Good Morning Sunshine! Make it a Day of Being Uncomfortable! We know that no one enjoys being uncomfortable. Yet it seems as though the times in life when we experience discomfort are the times that we learn, grow, and gather the strength to face fears and obstacles the most. Being uncomfortable often defines or develops our character. When we start a new endeavor, whether it be a new job, a new relationship, or a new life experience, it's not always easy. Yet when you face them head-on and look back, you see how a brief period of being uncomfortable has blessed your life. If you remain comfortable, you may never take risks to live fully, to love fully, to give fully, or to be fully the person God created you to be. Embrace the uncomfortable and Enjoy!

November 9

Good Morning Sunshine! Make it a Day of Remembering It's a New Day! New days mean new opportunities for fresh starts and a chance to change perspective and attitude. We often come to the end of a day and then continue to hang onto it, especially the ones where we wish we had made better choices or done, said, lived differently. Even though the day has ended, we continue to relive it or replay it in our minds over and over like we can go back and change it. Learn from yesterday and all your yesterdays but don't allow them to hold you captive and prevent you from living in the present! Take a deep breath, hold your head up high and let go of yesterday so you can live fully today! It's a New Day. Enjoy!

November 10

Good Morning Sunshine! Make it a Day of Making Your Words and Actions Match! Have you ever heard the words 'I love you' or 'Have a great day' through clenched teeth? Have you ever spoken them like that to someone? They don't have quite the same meaning or seem as authentic as when a smile is involved and the words flow freely from the lips. Have you ever witnessed someone who speaks one way, yet their actions don't match their words? Has this ever been you? Our words have a great impact on others, whether we speak in love or in anger. Our actions can affect those around us both positively and negatively. When used together, words and actions have incredible power and can change the world or at least your small part of it. Use them both wisely; to love, to encourage, to reach out, to make a difference. Let your words and actions match for goodness sake, and Enjoy!

November 11

Good Morning Sunshine! Make it a Day of Singing! I know, I know, it is early, and maybe you don't feel like singing. But for thousands of years, singing has been used as a form of expression of feelings and emotions. Singing is a means of lamenting and mourning. Singing is a way to celebrate or to praise and worship, or even a form of prayer. Psalm 95:1-2 says: "Come, let's sing out loud to the Lord! Let's raise a joyful shout to the rock of our salvation! Let's come before him with thanks. Let's shout songs of joy to him!" Singing has been a reminder of special moments, and it has mended broken hearts or celebrated joyful moments in life. Singing has a way of uniting people in a way nothing else can. Yip Harburg said: "Words make you think. Music makes you feel. A song makes you feel a thought." Feel your thoughts today. Sing to celebrate, sing to heal, sing to remind you of life's joys and blessings. Sing , and maybe others will join you in your song! Enjoy!

November 12

Good Morning Sunshine! Make it a Day of Finding Your Kid Again! Somewhere along the line, most of us have grown up, matured, or at the very least gotten older because we had no choice. However, many of us, due to life experience, have lost our kid-like qualities. We no longer have a sense of wonder or imagination and our ability to dream. We just face reality, get the facts and move along. We've lost our naivety and innocence and have become cynical and suspect of everyone and everything. We've lost our acceptance of others and traded it in for judgment. We've forgotten to play and laugh and not take life so seriously. Well, somewhere inside of you is 'your kid' , and today, your mission is to find it; dream, imagine, be silly, laugh, love, accept others and hope for an awesome future! Find your kid, and Enjoy!

November 13

Good Morning Sunshine! Make it a Day of Facing the Truth! The truth is you are alive today, and you get to enjoy the beauty of the earth and participate in living life. The truth is you have been created with meaning and purpose, with value. Proverbs 16:4 says: "God made everything with a place and a purpose…." Ask yourself the truth, do I live like I've been created with meaning and purpose, with value? The truth is God loves you more than you can ever imagine, and there's nothing you can do about it! You have been created to love and be loved. The truth is no one has the ability to make you feel inferior or less than unless you allow them to. The truth is you are a child of God and that alone should make you confident in who you are. Face the truth today; you are alive, you are a child of God, you have purpose and meaning, and you are loved. It's all true. Live like it and Enjoy!

November 14

Good Morning Sunshine! Make it a day of Being a Hero! We all have this idea of what a hero is; someone who is brave enough to run in and rescue people from a burning building, saving a damsel in distress, firefighters, policemen, the military, or anyone but us. I believe each of us is a hero. Christopher Reeve said: "A hero is an ordinary individual who finds the strength to persevere and endure in spite of overwhelming obstacles." I'm sure in your lifetime, you have come face to face with overwhelming obstacles. When you first faced them, you had no idea how you would overcome them but looking back, you realize you made it through to the other side. Your strength and perseverance made you a hero in your own life and perhaps inspired others along the way. A hero is one who believes in hope because believing in hope means all things are possible. Be hopeful, be a hero, and Enjoy!

November 15

Good Morning Sunshine! Make it a Day to Accept A Dare! Remember playing truth or dare as a kid? Me too...I always took the dare and often found myself in a little trouble or doing something I didn't want to do, but who can turn down a dare? I'm hoping you can't because I'm daring you today! I dare you to look in the mirror and say something positive about yourself and repeat it several times throughout the day. I dare you to smile as much as possible. I dare you to sing out loud, and I dare you to dance at least once today. Singing and dancing alone count but it's way more fun if you do them with others. I dare you to give compliments freely to as many people as possible. I dare you to be bold in your faith and share it with others...use your voice if you have to. I dare you to say I love you to all whom you love today and share the love of God with everyone! I dare you to laugh and be silly; be a kid again! I dare you to keep your eyes open for those in need and then do all you can to help. I dare you to pray for others and yourself. I dare you to accept my dare! Enjoy!!

November 16

Good Morning Sunshine! Make it a Day of Following Your Dreams! To follow dreams, you need to have them. Do you have dreams or know what your dreams are for the future? It was easy to dream as a child, but somehow, reality comes in and takes over, and we either forget to dream, or we're afraid to. Dreams require hard work to make them happen, and you have to risk the possibility of them not coming true the way you want them to. In order for anything in life to become a reality, it has to start with a thought, an idea, or a dream. Dreaming means you have hope in possibilities. Possibilities mean you have a desire. Desire will move you to action, and action will make your dreams come true! What do you want for your life? Follow your dreams! Dream big and work hard to make them happen. Following your dreams is worth the risk! Enjoy!

November 17

Good Morning Sunshine! Make it a Day of Speaking Up! How many times have you let a moment pass by where you wanted to say something but didn't? How many times have you replayed conversations, circumstances, and situations over and over in your mind and then told yourself, "I wish I had said this or that?" It could have been I love you, thank you, yes, no, I'm sorry, let's get together, can I have your number, you're beautiful, or words spoken to stand up for yourself, for others, or for social justice issues. Mitch Albom said: "Nothing haunts us like things we don't say." We are always afraid of what others might think of us, so we remain quiet and spend our time wishing we weren't so scared. Use your words wisely as they hold incredible power to harm or heal, to lift up or tear down, to spread anger or love and joy. Proverbs 18:4 says: "Wise words are like deep waters; wisdom flows from the wise like a bubbling brook." Use your power of voice wisely so that they might speak life and love. Speak Up and Enjoy!

November 18

Good Morning Sunshine! Make it a Day of Asking What, Where, How, When & Why! So often, we go through life and we never question anything when in reality, we should question everything. Questioning is how we learn and grow. Questioning does not mean you have free reign to be rude or disrespectful; there's never a time for that. What questioning means is that you have the desire to gain knowledge, learn more, to become more so that you can do more. The point of questioning is so that you can make a difference, that you have an understanding of your place in humanity, so you can live fully in a relationship with God, others, and the world around you. If you see something happening, ask what's going on, why is it happening, where do I fit in, what can I do, and how can I be of service, be a solution or be of help? Ask questions. Perhaps you'll be part of the answer! Enjoy!

November 19

Good Morning Sunshine! Make it a Day of Eunoia! I guess to make it a day of Eunoia, then you would need to know what Eunoia is. Eunoia means beautiful thinking. So make it a day of beautiful thinking. Have you ever consciously thought beautifully? We become what we think. If we think beautifully, our lives reflect beauty. If we think otherwise, our lives show that too. I am certain that if you intentionally considered beautiful thoughts, then beauty, joy, hope, love, and happiness would manifest in your life. You would see people in a more beautiful and positive light. You would see beauty in relationships with family, friends, and loved ones. You would see beauty in the world around you. We are bombarded with so many things in life that will dominate our thoughts with negativity, stress, and worry, but you can choose to challenge your thoughts and choose beautiful thinking! Choose Eunoia and Enjoy!!!

November 20

Good Morning Sunshine! Make it a Day Where Nothing is Sure! That sounds a bit frightening, doesn't it? After all, we like certainty and assurance. We like to be organized and in control. When life is uncertain, we often allow fears to take over, so why would we want our day to be one where nothing is sure? Margaret Drabble said: "When nothing is sure, everything is possible." In reality, nothing in life is sure or certain, yet possibilities are endless! Possibilities are only hindered by our fears and most often by our own self-inflicted limitations. Scripture tells us that with God, all things are possible. Imagine what your life could be or would be if you believed this and lived it! When you face uncertainty, when you have more questions than answers, when nothing seems sure, look for the possibilities, they do exist!! Live like nothing's sure and everything's possible, and Enjoy!

November 21

Good Morning Sunshine! Make it a Day of Significance! We often begin and end our days without recognizing the importance that each day holds. We overlook the potential we have to be relevant and to make an impact in the lives of others. We sometimes get caught up in a "what about me" attitude and don't grasp the concept of what can I do, what can I give or how can I make a difference. Nelson Mandela said: "What counts in life is not the mere fact that we have lived. It is what difference we have made to the lives of others that will determine the significance of the life we lead." You touch more lives than you will ever know. You have limitless potential to make a difference to many people. A smile, a positive attitude, a compassionate heart, hands that are willing to reach out or clasp in prayer, words that will lift up and encourage, perseverance , and determination in every situation. These are a few ways you can impact those around you! Make a difference! Live a Significant life and Enjoy!

November 22

Good Morning Sunshine! Make it a Day of Watching! Lao Tzo said: "Watch your thoughts; they become words. Watch your words; they become actions. Watch your actions; they become your character. Watch your character; it becomes your destiny." We don't often think that our thoughts will develop our character and become our destiny; it just happens. When we think, our thoughts usually don't remain in our mind, and if our thoughts don't come out verbally, they are often demonstrated in other ways. As a result, we may begin to act in a manner that reflects what we are thinking. Our anger or frustration will be reflected in our actions, but so will our joy, our love, and our generosity. Our thoughts, and our actions, will determine our course. Obviously, the outward display of our actions shows our character and shapes our lives. The beauty of this process is that our thoughts can be what we want them to be. Not every thought will be a happy one. However, no matter what is going on in the world and in your own life, the one thing you can control is your thoughts, and you know where that leads! Challenge your own thoughts today. You have that power. Philippians 4:8 says: "And now, dear brothers and sisters, one final thing. Fix your thoughts on what is true, and honorable, and right, and pure, lovely, and admirable. Think about things that are excellent and worthy of praise." If your thoughts need redirecting, pray, and look to God to guide you so that your character is shaped by God. Think positive thoughts; think about those things that are right, pure, and admirable. Think about love! Then allow these to become your actions and your character. Watch your thoughts and Enjoy!

November 23

Good Morning Sunshine! Make it a Day of Making It Happen! What is it? It's your life; make your life happen! We can't just talk about wanting things or experiences to take place in our lives; we have to go out and make things and experiences happen! We can think and ponder and dream, but until we actually do something to create, our thoughts, ponderings, and dreams may not come true. You make it happen; you create your life! By all means, pray about it and for it. However, put your prayers into action. I read once that we should participate in answering our own prayers. Ask God for strength to empower you but then go be part of the answer; make it happen! If you don't like your life and circumstances, change it. If you can't change it, change your attitude toward it. Either way, you have a choice how to live it, how to make it happen & how to experience it. Live well, live in peace, love, and hope! Make IT happen, and Enjoy!

November 24

Good Morning Sunshine! Happy Thanksgiving! Make it a day to give thanks for the people in your life; for those whom you will spend this day with, for those that are far from you in the distance but close in heart & spirit, for those who have touched your life for just a brief moment in time & for those who have been a presence for a lifetime. Give thanks to those you've lost, yet somehow, they still bless you. Give thanks to those whom you are unaware of the effect they have on your life, but without them, things wouldn't be the same. Give thanks to those who encourage & support you, to those who challenge you and help you grow, to those who make you laugh or wipe your tears. Give thanks for what's most important in your life, people and relationships. You see, it's the relationships, the encounters with others, that give life meaning & value. Stuff is great & you can be thankful for that as well, but without relationships, stuff just doesn't have the same meaning! Look around, take it all in. No matter your circumstances, there is so much to be thankful for. See your blessings, embrace them, give thanks to God & Enjoy! p.s. I AM THANKFUL FOR YOU!!!

November 25

Good Morning Sunshine! Make it a Day of Gentleness! How blessed we would be if we lived, realizing the importance of being gentle to others and to ourselves. Perhaps I have that in the reverse order. Maybe, just maybe, we are supposed to be gentle to ourselves so that we can be gentler to others. We have no problem being harsh and beating ourselves up in our own minds. How often have you thought negatively about yourself or compared yourself to someone else, elevating them and lowering your own self-image? Have you put yourself down or been your own worst inner critic? Well, even if you try to hide it, how you treat yourself can very easily be passed on to others. The second greatest commandment is to love your neighbor as yourself. So to love others fully, you really should do your very best to love yourself! To be truly kind to others, you should be kind to yourself! To share genuine peace and joy and gentleness, it's important to have peace and joy and gentleness within you, for you. Be blessed today. Be kind to yourself and share kindness with others. Love you, love others. Be gentle to yourself and pass it on and Enjoy!

November 26

Good Morning Sunshine! Make it a day of Daring Adventure! Helen Keller said: "Life is either a daring adventure or nothing at all." How awesome it would be if we faced each day as though it were an adventure! We would see things so differently. We might even try new things, new foods, or experiences. We might be brave enough to go to new places and meet new people. The best part is that you can do this without traveling the world. However, if you have the opportunity to travel the world, do it!!! Be adventurous today! Try driving to or from work a different way. Take a more scenic route and take in things you haven't noticed before. Go to a new restaurant or make a new recipe and learn about different cultures. Smile, make eye contact , and say hello to everyone. Everyday life is a beautiful, daring adventure with so many opportunities to live! Don't be afraid to try new things! Be alive, embrace the adventure of life and Enjoy!

November 27

Good Morning Sunshine! Make it a Day of Valuing Time! When our schedules are full, and life is busy, we don't have enough time. When we are bored and looking for things to do, we have too much time. We have all given time to those who may not have appreciated it, and probably, at one point, we have wasted someone else's time. We have done all of these things, most likely, without considering the true value of each moment. Why? Because we believe there will be the next moment, and we often take time for granted. The best gift we can ever give or receive is the gift of time. There is nothing more precious. Live every moment appreciating the time you have been given. Give thanks for the time that others give to you. Breathe it all in. Embrace it. Share it with others! Give your time whenever possible. Make every second count! Value time and Enjoy!

November 28

Good Morning Sunshine! Make it a Day of Calculating Your Happiness! Have you ever done that? I would bet that most of us haven't. Why are we so good at counting our troubles and woes and adding up the ways we have been wronged but we rarely take the opportunity to add up joys and happiness? Perhaps some don't calculate happiness because they believe they have nothing to add up. William Feather said: "Plenty of people miss their share of happiness, not because they never found it, but because they didn't stop to enjoy it." We are all given so many blessings and opportunities to find happiness, but we often forget to take account of the goodness of life. We have a God who loves us. We are gifted with the very air we breathe, the people we love and those who love us in return, and our ability to live with meaning and purpose. Circumstances can be less than ideal at times, but life is always, always, always good! You have the option to count your troubles or calculate your happiness. Whichever one you choose to focus on will add up much faster. Focus on blessings, joys & happiness...lose count, start again and Enjoy!

November 29

Good Morning Sunshine! Make it a Day of Not Judging Others! This is a hard one because we judge whether we mean to or not. We tend to see the outside and judge one another by our weight, hairstyle, and clothing. After all, clothes make the man (or woman). We judge vocations, cars, homes, and possessions. We even judge the lifestyles of others when we think they're not living the way we deem as appropriate or acceptable. What we don't realize is that while we're judging others, someone is judging us. Mother Teresa said: "If you judge people, then you have no time to love them." We weren't created to judge but to love. You may not like everyone you encounter, but you are called to love them like Christ anyway. We can't help what others do, but we can choose to live in the manner in which we've been called; to love. See others as Christ would. Let God be the judge so that you have plenty of time to love! Stop judging and get busy loving! Enjoy!

November 30

Good Morning Sunshine! Make it a Day of Replacing Negative Thoughts! I suppose that's just another way of saying think positive! Our thoughts are so important; they dictate our moods, our actions or inactions and life direction, our decisions, our relationships with God, others, and ourselves. If our thinking is negative, so will be our attitude on living; they go hand in hand. The opposite is also true. If you replace negative thinking with positive thinking, then you begin to live in a positive light, and sooner or later, the results are bound to be positive! If we change our thoughts from "I give up, nothing's ever good, and it's too late" to "I'll never, never, never give up, I'm going to find good in this everything, and there's still hope," we might actually begin to see some change in the world and in ourselves. Replace the negative thoughts with positive thoughts; allow the change to begin, and Enjoy!

December

December 1

Good Morning Sunshine! Make it a Day of Remembering the Reason for the Season! The last few weeks have been full; full of shopping for the perfect gifts and the perfect meals, full of planning and preparation, full of going to holiday gatherings, zoom meetings, and special events, and spending time with family, friends, and loved ones. For some, it's just been a time of year to get through because circumstances have made it difficult to celebrate. Whether we're happy and looking forward to the season's festivities or we're looking for a new start in the new year and leaving this one behind, this season can be full and overwhelming. No matter what you've experienced or how you're feeling, it's important to stop, take a deep breath and focus on the true meaning of Christmas; the Hope, Peace, Love, and Joy of Jesus Christ.! "For to us a child is born, to us a Son is given and the government will rest upon his shoulders. And he will be called Wonderful Counselor, Might God, Everlasting Father, Prince of Peace." (Isaiah 9:6). Remember the True Reason for the Season, allow Jesus Christ to be born in you, and Enjoy!

December 2

Good Morning Sunshine! Make it a Day of "Carbonated Holiness!" What is carbonated holiness, you ask? Anne Lamott says its laughter. Think about this, when you shake a can of soda and then open it, what happens? It explodes everywhere! That's what happens when you laugh; it's as though your joy has been shaken up and released; then it can't help but splash onto others. Did you ever hear someone laugh, and suddenly you're laughing, but you have no idea why? It's contagious; You can't help it! You've been splashed with joy! Did you ever find yourself in a serious situation, and, while it may be on the border of being inappropriate, suddenly find yourself laughing so hard? The build-up was just too much, the top was popped, and laughter brought about so much relief. Laughing is healing and bonding. People who laugh together touch and talk and actually look at one another! Be carbonated holiness, splash the world with laughter and Enjoy!

December 3

Good Morning Sunshine! Make it a Day of Hope! Today is filled with more than 24 hours. Today contains more than morning, noon, and night. Today has all the potential in the world to be beautiful, amazing, and blessed. Our expectations for this day and every day should be overflowing with hope and endless possibilities. We seem to believe that our days are only full of our circumstances, challenges, or our struggles, and it becomes difficult to see anything, especially hope and potential. Circumstances will not always make us feel good or feel like there is hope, but this is where faith should step in and take over. Faith provides vision far beyond what's directly in front of us to what can be. Faith reassures us of God's promises to never leave us nor forsake us. Faith, through Scripture, reminds us that our God has plans for us, for YOU! Plans for good to give you a future and hope. (Jeremiah 29:11). Don't cave to your feelings. Don't become your circumstances; live your faith! Be strengthened by your faith and see beyond your circumstances. Choose to fill today with Hope and Enjoy!

December 4

Good Morning Sunshine! Make it a Day of Speaking IT Aloud and Often! Believe that this new day will be a good one! Speak it aloud and often throughout the day! Know that you are a beautiful creation of God designed with meaning and a unique purpose. Believe that you can and do make the world a better place. Yes, YOU! Then speak it aloud and often! Our words can hinder us from moving forward, or they can propel us and keep us going in the right direction. How we speak to and about others also has a direct effect on us. How we speak about ourselves can truly make us or break us. Choose to encourage, lift up, see the good in you, the world, and others, then share it! Speak it aloud and often! What is IT? It is goodness, joy, love, compassion, praise, forgiveness, encouragement, support, hope, and words that bring light, love, and life! Speak them all to yourself and others, aloud and often, and Enjoy!!!

December 5

Good Morning Sunshine! Make it a Day of Surprising Yourself! Neil Gaiman said: "May your coming year be filled with magic and dreams and good madness. I hope you read some fine books and kiss someone who thinks you're wonderful, and don't forget to make some art-write or draw or build or sing or live as only you can. And I hope somewhere in the next year, you surprise yourself." You have such amazing ability and potential to live, really live, a full, productive, adventurous, love filled and joyful life! Many will say that circumstances won't allow it, but the truth is, the only thing holding us back, is us! Surprise yourself and live not as a person of circumstances, but a person of faith and hope. Your circumstances may not change, but your attitude and how you face them can! Read, love, kiss, embrace, write, draw, build, sing, live only as you can! Surprise yourself and Enjoy!

December 6

Good Morning Sunshine! Make it a Day of Spreading Light! Edith Wharton said: "There are two ways of spreading light: to be the candle or the mirror that reflects it." Each of us has the ability to spread light, to shine with joy, to light to the world with a positive attitude, to share the light of Christ, and offer the world a glimmer of hope. We can choose to be on fire with a flame that will light the path for others and extend warmth to those in need. Who knows, maybe they will catch fire too. Or we can allow our flame to grow dim. We can choose to reflect the light of the love of God within us or keep it to ourselves. Jesus said in John 8:12: "I have come into the world as light so that whoever believes in me may not remain in darkness." I understand that life can be hard, and that's probably an understatement. I know there are some who find it difficult to keep a flame burning, but I believe we all have a choice whether to let our light grow stronger and spread it to others or allow it to be extinguished. If your candle is dim, look for the light in others around you to help you shine until you burn brightly again. Only you can determine to keep the flame burning or not. You only live once; why not do it as a candle, shine light, spread light!! Shine and Enjoy!

December 7

Good Morning Sunshine! Make it a Day of Choosing Love as a Way of Life! Did you ever notice that people make resolutions to change their lives in some way, shape, or form; I'm going to exercise and lose weight, get more organized, quit smoking, and live with less stress. You name a way to change, and it's someone's resolution, maybe even yours. The track record for keeping up with resolutions is not so good. What we're doing is pointing out our flaws and bad habits and looking for a change from a negative perspective. Why not begin from a place of positivity? If you choose love as a way of life, it can be much more powerful than making a resolution that most won't keep up with. Wake up and choose to love! First, Love God. Loving God will keep you focused and strengthen you to accomplish any dream or goal before you and give you peace on top of it. Love others unconditionally! This will alleviate stress and keep you mindful that you're not alone. It might even prompt you to see the needs of others and then do something about it, which can lead to helping you feel great. Love you! When you love yourself, it will help you care for yourself, body, mind, and spirit. Loving yourself improves your self-esteem, helps your determination and perseverance, and motivates you to maintain a positive mindset. When you love yourself, you'll take care of yourself. Do you want a positive change? Choose love as a way of life, and Enjoy!

December 8

Good Morning Sunshine! Make it a Day Worth Watching! You know the expression "my life flashed before my eyes." Well, if that were to happen and your life flashed before your eyes, would you like what you saw? Would you see that you lived in a way that made you realize that life is precious and way too short? Did you use your time wisely and live life to its fullest? Were you happy for yourself and for others, or did you spend too much time harboring feelings of anger and hanging onto grudges? Did you celebrate and rejoice and embrace all of life; blessings, challenges, relationships, obstacles or did you allow these moments to be taken for granted or to fall by the wayside? Here's the thing, your life is still in progress, and you have the opportunity every single day to make your "life flashes" worth watching! Get going!! Life is too short so do something about it! Live happy and be happy for others! Live love and share the love with others! You get to determine your flashes; make them bright, beautiful, and worth watching! Enjoy!

December 9

Good Morning Sunshine! Make it a Day of Making a Contribution! Have you ever given thought to what you contribute to the world or to your community or to charity or to your relationships with God, family, friends, or loved ones? Have you ever just thought, "what is it that I can give or be a part of today, or how can I make a difference?" I think, as a whole, most ask "what can I get" so much more than "what can I give or contribute." Noora Ahmed Alsuwaidi said: "People who don't take things for granted are the ones who know the value of contributing and sharing in life. Feeling grateful to the blessings around you makes you a person with a living heart who can appreciate God's blessings, enjoy life, and feel the responsibility towards others too."

Believe it or not, our calling, our purpose, our gifts, and our talents, our love, none of them belong to us. They are a part of us that we are meant to share, to give away, to contribute to the world. We are created to be in a relationship with God, nature, and with each other. If we all kept that in mind and asked ourselves, "What can I contribute to these relationships?" no one would be lacking anything. Ask what you can give or be a part of today! Share you, give you, contribute to you and watch the world, or at least your part of the world, transform! Enjoy!

December 10

Good Morning Sunshine! Make it a Day of Making Mistakes!! I know you are not going to like this because no one likes to make mistakes, to do the wrong thing or to fail. I don't like it either except for this... when you make mistakes, it means that you are doing something, trying something, learning something! We have learned by trial and error since we were born, but somewhere along the line, it has become unacceptable and embarrassing. Just think of all the things you would try, or try again, if you weren't afraid to make mistakes! You might actually keep trying until things go the way you want them to, or you learn a better way. Go do something, try something, learn something, and don't be afraid to make mistakes. Believe there is no such thing as failure. If you tried and it didn't go as planned, as long as you don't give up, and you have learned something, then you haven't failed. Go live and learn! Make mistakes and Enjoy!

December 11

Good Morning Sunshine! Make it a Day of Getting In Shape! This doesn't necessarily mean to start physically working out but to change, mold, or shape your life the way you want it to be. I read a quote that said: "This is your world. Shape it, or someone else will." Do you realize that you get to determine the shape of your life? If you don't like the current shape, then change it to what you want it to be. It's not always easy. When a potter has clay on a wheel, they take their time carefully molding the clay until the desired shape is formed. When the clay doesn't take on the intended shape, the potter starts over. The clay is squeezed, pressed upon, and molded until it comes out just right. It may take time to shape your life exactly how you want it. You may feel the squeezing and pressure while the molding and shaping process is happening. But the key is to keep going or starting over until your shape, your life, is what you want it to be! Get in shape, the shape you want, and Enjoy!

December 12

Good Morning Sunshine! Make it a Day of Having an Increasingly Grateful Heart! What is it that you are grateful for in your life? Is it the food you eat or the roof over your head, the job that pays the bills, or the technology that allows you to read my daily ramblings? Are you grateful for the relationships in your life and the time you get to spend with those you love and care about? Are you grateful that there are those who love you in return? Are you grateful for God and the faith and blessings that you have received or blessings that you have been a part of giving to others? Are you grateful for the world around you and the air you breathe, and the breath you just took? Are you grateful to be alive? Are you grateful for so much more than my finite list? I hope you said yes to all the above! It has been said that "those who live with increasingly grateful hearts have decreasingly complaining mouths. You can't possibly count all your blessings if your mouth and mind are complaining!" 1 Thessalonians 5:16-18 says: "Rejoice always, pray continually, give thanks in all circumstances; for this is God's will for you in Christ Jesus." The Good News is that God wants you to be happy, to pray to God, and to always be thankful for all the blessings in your life. Be Increasingly Grateful and watch your life change for the better, then live as an example that others may follow your lead and Enjoy!

December 13

Good Morning Sunshine! Make it a Day of Keeping Your Focus on God! Life can be so crazy sometimes, can't it? We're always being pulled one way or another and often distracted because of circumstances and everything that's vying for our attention; the news and social media, politics, work, home, family, and the list goes on. How can anyone keep their focus when life is so busy or stressful? Sometimes to move forward in life, it's important to take a step back and focus so you can determine who you are, where you are, where you want to be, and what exactly you are seeking, so you know what direction you are headed. Most of us live busy lifestyles, but it's important to understand the value of knowing what we are doing and why we are doing it. I don't know about you, but I've lived my life focused on God, and I've lived my life focused on circumstances, schedules and problems. Being focused on God is better! Isaiah 26:3 says: "You will keep in perfect peace all who trust in you, all whose thoughts are fixed on you!" When we focus on what is True and Right and Holy, when we focus on God, our lives are different. Our circumstances may not change. We will most likely still be busy, but we will be more peaceful, intentional, and filled with meaning and purpose. In your busyness and in spite of your circumstances, find perfect peace by keeping your focus on God and Enjoy!

December 14

Good Morning Sunshine! Make it a Day of Daring Something! Daring means to do something adventurous or audaciously bold. How great would it be if we lived with daring attitudes? Imagine the things you would do, the people you would meet, the experiences you would encounter! What if you dared to believe in yourself and your abilities and you tried new things? If you spend your life daring nothing, then nothing is what you may end up with. I dare you to do something daring, not crazy or unsafe, but daring nonetheless! I dare you to love unconditionally! I dare you to walk a familiar path and notice new things along your journey. I dare you to get back up when you're down! I dare you to laugh and not take life so seriously! I dare you to find joy in simple pleasures. I dare you to find someone in need and help them. I dare you to express your faith, not necessarily by your words, but in your actions. I dare you to forgive. I dare you to hope! I dare you to break free from fears and live a full life. Be adventurous and audaciously bold! Dare something and Enjoy!

December 15

Good Morning Sunshine! Make it a Day of Releasing Your Inner Summer!! Albert Camus wrote, "In the depth of winter, I finally learned that within me there lay an invincible summer." In the summer, there is warmth and sunshine. We dress lighter, open our windows and get out much more often. Our spirits seem a bit freer. Obviously, these things are much easier to do when the weather is warmer, but there's nothing preventing us from releasing the warmth and rays of light that are within us while we wait for the seasons to change. No matter the seasonal weather, within each of us lies an invincible summer that we just need to release. Others can feel warmth in our presence or in our words and actions. The rays of our hope and faith in God have the potential to shine from us if we release them. Our spirits can be lighter and freer if we choose to trust God with our fears, worries, and burdens. No matter what is happening outside, choose to believe in and live as though your inner summer is invincible, and Enjoy!

December 16

Good Morning Sunshine! Make it a Day of Being an Essential Ingredient! Do you realize the potential you possess to add part of you to the world and to all of those in it? Your gifts and talents, coupled with your love, mercy, joy, generosity, compassion, encouragement, and hope (add your own thoughts here), could be the precise ingredients that someone else may need to be added to their lives? Although circumstances can be difficult, Life is beautiful, and there is always hope. Sometimes we just need to be reminded of that; sometimes, we need to be the reminders! You were created with meaning and purpose. You are here to add something to this world. You are an essential ingredient in life! Matthew 5:13(MSG) says: "Let me tell you why you are here. You're here to be salt-seasoning that brings out the God-flavors of this earth. If you lose your saltiness, how will people taste godliness?" What flavor will you add to the world today? What will you add to your relationships? You are an essential ingredient! Just add you and Enjoy!

December 17

Good Morning Sunshine! Make it a Day of Realizing What You Have! Most of us have a list of wants and desires in life. That is great because they should prompt us to work hard to pursue our goals until they are achieved. Very often though, we live wanting, obtaining, discarding, and then wanting more. The truth is that we will never be content in getting what we want until we are content with what we have. It is when we realize how blessed we are with our relationships, our surroundings, and our "stuff" that we are truly happy and content. Socrates said: "He who is not contented with what he has, would not be content with what he would like to have." And the Scriptures tell us in 1 Timothy 6:6: "True godliness with contentment is itself great wealth." Being content doesn't mean you always get what you want. Contentment is when you realize and are thankful for, what you already have. You are blessed! Realize what you have, be content, and Enjoy!

December 18

Good Morning Sunshine! Make it a Day of Making A Good Life!
Ward Foley said: "We are not given a good life or a bad life. We are
given life. And it's up to you to make it good or bad." There's not a
person alive who hasn't had bad things happen to them.
Unfortunately, it is part of life. However, how we handle these
things or choose to face our situations determines if we make it a
good life or a bad life. The great part is we get to choose! We may
not get to choose some of our life circumstances, but we can choose
how to face them, and we can choose to make something good come
from everything. If you want a good life, you can have it! It will
require hard work, taking responsibility, determination, and
perseverance, along with a good attitude and an abundance of
prayer, faith, and hope. Circumstances may not always be good, but
life is! Life is always, always, always good! Choose to see it that
way! Choose to live it that way! Choose to make it that way! Make
it a good life, and Enjoy!

December 19

Good Morning Sunshine! Make it a Day To Keep on Dancing! Some people hate to dance because they think they don't know how or they don't want to look foolish in front of others. Others love to dance and feel it is a passion and an art. While there are those, who dance at events with family and friends and are happy dancing and celebrating life and couldn't care less about what they look like or who is watching. Then others just like to dance to the beat and music in their own minds. We have all heard the saying: "Dance like no one's watching," but I have read somewhere that we should look up to the people who keep on dancing even after the music stops because those are the people who will keep on trying even after all hope seems lost. I think if you can keep dancing, no matter what's going on, then hope is all you have and perhaps exactly what you need. So break out in a little spontaneous dancing today. You might just be the music and the glimmer of hope that someone else needs to see and hear to make them dance. You might just remind yourself to always have hope as well! Keep Dancing and Enjoy!

December 20

Good Morning Sunshine! Make it a Day of God Counting On You! Yesterday in church, we sang a Pete Seeger song, "God's Counting on Me, God's Counting on You," and it's been resonating in my mind since. I've heard it before; God's counting on you, but every once in a while, it's good to be reminded. As you go through life, you might think that your families and friends count on you. Certainly, your employers count on you to come to work and perform well. Others have expectations of you; they count on you for many things, but what if you lived believing that God is counting on you? Would you live differently? Would you treat people the way God wants you to or the way you feel like treating them? Would you love everyone and see God everywhere and in everything? Well, my friends, God is counting on YOU! You have been entrusted to care for the earth; how are you doing with that? You have been commanded to love God and to love your neighbor as yourself; how's that going? God is counting on YOU...live like it and Enjoy!

December 21

Good Morning Sunshine! Make it a Day of Being the Reason Someone Smiles! I read this on a Facebook post and thought it was awesome! What if your intention today was to do whatever you could to make someone else smile? It probably wouldn't take much. I bet if you smiled first, someone would eventually smile in response. What if you called a friend or family member out of the blue to let them know that you just wanted to hear their voice? I bet they'd smile. What if you committed a random act of kindness or helped someone in need or shared an encouraging word, or were a listening ear? There are endless possibilities that provide you an opportunity to be the reason someone else smiles today! Smiles bring joy and light. If you smile, you'll offer joy and light! So get out there and smile like you mean it! Your smile, your joy, and your light can be the reason someone else will smile. And their smile may be the cause of others to smile... you could start a smiling chain reaction! Do it! Be the reason for causing some joy in the world, and Enjoy!!

December 22

Good Morning Sunshine! Make it a Day of Greater Than! Remember the math problems greater than >/< less than? Wouldn't it be awesome if we applied the same concept to our lives by saying and believing things like my faith is greater than my fears? I am greater than my circumstances! Love is greater than hatred. Acceptance of others is greater than judgment and rejection. Giving really is greater than receiving. I am greater than any obstacle or challenge before me. My confidence is greater than my self-doubt. My God is greater than my problems! Abdul Kalam said, "As a child of God, I am greater than anything that can happen to me." Change your way of thinking from less than to greater than! You are a child of God... God's love for you is greater than you can imagine! Live it, believe it! Be greater than and Enjoy!

December 23

Good Morning Sunshine! Make it a Day of Being First! This shouldn't be too difficult because we are encouraged to be first, number one. We are taught to be the best from a very early age. It is enforced over time as we are to look out for number one. And who is number one? We are, of course. Today I am going to continue to encourage you to strive to be first, but perhaps to be first in a different way. Be first to have a positive attitude. Be first to share your love of God. Be the first to reach out when someone is in need. Be first to offer prayer. Be first to humble yourself before God. James 4:10 says: "Humble yourselves before the Lord, and he will exalt you." Be the first to share your gifts and talents. Be the first to offer words of kindness, joy, and support. Be the first to say I am sorry and the first to offer forgiveness. Be the first to smile. Be the first to listen. Be the first to stand up for a good cause. Be the first to speak out against social injustice. Be the first to say thank you. Be the first to share your blessings with others. Be the first to sing and dance and invite others to join you. Be the first to show compassion and mercy. Be the first to share your resources. Be first to open your arms to embrace others. Be the first to love! Go be first today. Be first to live as an example of Jesus Christ that others will follow! You are number one! Enjoy!!

December 24

Good Morning Sunshine! Make it a Day of Opportunity! We have such limited sight sometimes, don't we? Why is it that our vision usually sees only what's around us? We have no problem seeing things like our own circumstances, challenges, and obstacles. Why can't we use our vision to see beyond our struggles or to see our difficulties as opportunities? The only difference between an obstacle and an opportunity is our attitude. In the wise words of Captain Jack Sparrow: "The problem is not the problem. The problem is your attitude about the problem." Life is not always easy. In fact, sometimes life is downright hard. So, you have a choice to see problems and obstacles and allow them to hinder you. You might even use them as an excuse to harbor bad feelings and express negative thoughts. Or, you can have the vision to see beyond what's in front of you and see what can be. You have the power to make everything, yes everything, an opportunity! Psalm 34:10 says: "Those who trust in the Lord will lack no good thing." Don't just see today. Trust God and have vision! Seize everything as an opportunity and Enjoy!

December 25

Merry Christmas Sunshine! Make it a Day of Lots..... Enjoy your family and friends, lots! Celebrate life! Love lots, Give lots, Laugh lots, Hug lots, Eat lots, Pray lots....Give lots of thanks to God for it all! God loves you, lots!! God gave you lots in the many gifts and blessings in your life, be sure to embrace the greatest gift of all, Jesus, Lots!!! Let the gift of Christ live in you and through you lots that others may know this love which you have found and Enjoy!!! P.S. I love you all, lots! Thank you for the gift of allowing me to share my daily thoughts and prayers with you!! You bless me! Yup, you got it...lots! xo

December 26

Good Morning Sunshine! Make it a Day of Having a Playful Spirit. Remember what it was like to be a kid? Life was fun, and laughing was easy. Remember when we could make anything fun and be silly and laugh? Remember it being okay that we were silly in the first place? Remember when our first thought was to love and to trust those around us and not automatically assume there were ulterior motives involved? Remember when race, class, culture, and gender didn't matter because we saw and accepted everyone for who they were, well, except for the occasional boy/girl cooties thing. Remember, as kids, we were innocent and pure in heart before we were jaded by the world, and we were so resilient. If we fell down, we would brush ourselves off and start again. If someone hurt our feelings, we were quick to forgive, be friends again, and move forward. When we were by ourselves, we would still play, skip, sing and not feel like we were all alone. When we heard music, we couldn't help ourselves, and we would start dancing wherever we were, no matter who was watching. We found fun, we made fun, and we had fun. Well, every day that goes by, it gets a little harder to remember these things, doesn't it? It becomes more difficult to find our playful spirit and to have fun, and to really enjoy life. Time, experience, people, and life has tired us out to some extent and taught us to live more cynical lives. God reminds us that we must become like children, not naïve or immature, but pure in heart, mind, and spirit. What if we started doing that again? Enjoying life, laughing, being lighthearted, letting things go, picking ourselves up after a fall, giggling, being silly, dancing…I could go on and on. I'm not advocating immaturity, but I'm strongly encouraging a playful, happy, joyful spirit. Imagine our days if we always held onto these childlike qualities? Less stress, more joy. I encourage you to find fun, make fun, have fun! Be a kid again! Have a playful spirit again! Love everyone, laugh, be silly, steer clear of cooties and Enjoy!

December 27

Good Morning Sunshine! Make it a Day of Being Generous! The definition of Generosity is unselfish giving or sharing, freedom from meanness or smallness of mind or character or abundance. We often associate generosity with money or material items. If you have it to give in order to help others in need, by all means, be generous in your giving, but there are so many ways to be generous. Be generous with your time. Time is the most precious gift you can give to someone. Time builds relationships, provides comfort and assurance, and offers healing. Your presence is a gift; give it generously. Be generous in listening and not speaking. Be generous with your laughter and joy. The world is in serious need of happiness, don't hang onto it; share it in abundance! Be generous in kindness; speak kind words, and do kind acts. Be generous with love. Give it away in abundance. Love is so valuable; share it with those who love you and those who may not, but don't keep it to yourself. Be generous with your life; give youself, your presence, your joy, your kindness, your love. You have it...share it!! Your generosity will change the world! Give and Enjoy!

December 28

Good Morning Sunshine! Make it a Day of Opening Every Door!
We have heard the saying, "When opportunity knocks, open the
door." Have you ever given much thought to this? It's implying that
you have to do something. You have to open the door! How many
times have you had the opportunity to knock, and you didn't answer
because of fear, unwillingness to get out of your comfort zone,
laziness, pride, or some other reason? And each time the door was
unopened, there were excellent excuses as to why you couldn't,
shouldn't, or wouldn't answer. Opportunity knocks all the time; the
doors of new relationships, the doors of hope, faith, and trust in God,
the doors of reaching out to those in need, the doors of new
experiences, the doors of giving of yourself to make a difference,
the doors of achieving goals. They are all knocking, and they are all
waiting to be opened. In the end, we only regret the unopened doors
and the chances not taken. Take a chance... open a
door! Opportunity is knocking; can't you hear it? Don't just sit
there... go open every door and Enjoy!!

December 29

Good Morning Sunshine! Make it a Day of Love! What if every day were a day of love? Robert Heinlein wrote, "Love is that condition in which the happiness of another is essential to your own." It would be amazing if we thought of love and lived love out this way. We all want to be happy, but we don't necessarily realize that true, unconditional love hinges on sharing happiness and joy with others. We tend to love others if they are like us, if they are not flawed in any way, or if they do what we want or live, behave and speak in ways that are acceptable to us and if they make us happy. But true, unconditional love is not loving others for their perfection but loving in spite of imperfections. Oh, and no one is perfect, not even you (or me)! If you expect to be loved unconditionally, then you must love unconditionally! If you want to be truly happy, then concern yourself with the happiness of others. Jesus said: "Love one another, love your enemies, love the Lord your God with all your heart, all your soul, all your strength and all your mind and love your neighbor as you love yourself." Love and happiness are connected. Love! Make the world a happier place, and Enjoy!

December 30

Good Morning Sunshine! Make it a Day to Lighten Up and Have Some Fun! Life can be pretty serious sometimes, can't it? It is not for the faint of heart. Circumstances are tough, problems surround us, obstacles keep appearing, and challenges seem to get more challenging. It is no wonder that we get caught up in seriousness. We forget to laugh, to lighten up, and to have some fun. What I have realized is that we are going to go through today no matter what, so we have two choices; we can worry, be fearful, miserable, and uncertain or we can have faith and give our worries, fears, and uncertainties to God and we can choose to lighten up, have some fun and perhaps gain some peace in the process. Mark Twain said: "Humor is mankind's greatest blessing" and "Against the assault of laughter, nothing can stand." Proverbs 17:22 says: "A joyful heart is good medicine." Laughter is healing to you and to those around you. Laughter can lighten a mood, eliminate negative emotions and even provide new insight and new direction. If this sounds silly to you, then you need a good laugh more than anyone. Life can be serious, but laughter will help you through it. Lighten up, have some fun and Enjoy!

December 31

Good Morning Sunshine! Make it a Day of Caring for Your Future Self!! Years ago, we never realized that decisions made would bring us to where we are today, but they did. So that means decisions we make now are shaping who we will continue to become. You may not have power over many things in life, but you do have power over your future self. Rick Hanson said, "Who is the one person you have the greatest power over? It is your future self. You hold that life in your hands, and what it will depend on how you care for it." So how are you caring for yourself today that your future self will thank you for in the future? Are you caring for yourself, body, mind, and spirit? Do you eat right and exercise to stay healthy and give your future self every opportunity to live a long, full life? Do you think positive thoughts or strive to learn as much as possible to keep your mind sharp? Do you pray and seek God in every aspect of your life? Do you live with hope? Are you living in a manner that is relevant to others around you? Will your future self look back and thank you for loving and caring for you and for others? Start caring for your future.

CPSIA information can be obtained
at www.ICGtesting.com
Printed in the USA
BVHW031649251022
650258BV00013B/361

9 781088 056349